The Balance
of Power
in the
Interwar Years

Studies in Political Science
Consulting Editor,
Inis L. Claude, Jr.
University of Michigan

The Balance of Power in the Interwar Years, 1919-1939

William J. Newman
Boston University

 **Random House**
New York

Quotation from *Exile and
Other Poems* by St.-John Perse.
Translated by Denis Devlin.
"Exile." Bollingen Series XV.
2nd edition, 1953. Distributed
by Pantheon Books. By
permission of Bollingen Foundation,
New York.

Design by William Rose

I have built upon the abyss and the spindrift and the sand-smoke. I shall lie down in cistern and hollow vessel,
   In all stale and empty places where lies the taste of greatness.
". . . There were fewer breezes to flatter the Julii; fewer alliances to assist the great priestly castes.
Where the sands go to their song, there go the Princes of exile,
Where there were high taut sails, there goes the wreck more silken than a lute-maker's dream,
Where there were great military actions, there lies whitening now the jawbone of an ass,
And the rounding sea rolls her noise of skulls on the shores,
And all things in the world to her are in vain, so we heard one night at the world's edge
From the wind's militias in the sands of exile . . ."

> ———From "Exile" by St.-John Perse
> (Alexis Saint-Léger Léger,
> Secretary General of the French
> Foreign Ministry, 1933–1940.
> Nobel Prize Winner for
> Literature, 1960).

To the Memory of My Mother

Preface

This book is a study in some depth of the balance of power through an analysis of a particular balance. It considers the establishment of a balance at Locarno and its collapse in the 1930's, an approach that serves several purposes. First, by demonstrating the complexities of balance of power politics, it makes it possible to move away from the simple or abstract formulations and rules that a theoretical study of international relations tends to establish, and aims to provide the student with a sense of the difficulties and the immense complexities of the actual process of trying to make a balance of power function. Such a study may be compared to the internship that follows theoretical training in a medical school. For just as in the field of medicine no one is a doctor or a research scientist until he has been brought face-to-face with the brute reality of medical work and the difficulties of applying theory to concrete cases, similarly in the study of the balance of power there is a need for bringing theory into some viable relationship to reality. Few concepts lend themselves so well to misleading simplification as balance of power. Adjust the weights here and there and, behold! the balance is still in balance. An analysis and understanding of the complex and terrible dilemmas in making the balance function properly will, it is hoped, destroy illusions about what such a process involves. Theory is of the essence, of course, but so is reality.

Second, this study aims to acquaint the student of political science with the interwar years and to bring him into contact with them in the context of the framework and concepts of political science. The interwar years are now history, and it is easy to pigeonhole them in some theoretical box. But it is useful for the political scientist to possess a better knowledge of this period than that necessary for the simplification that boxing must involve, for him to come into some contact with the excellent work that has been done by the historians on the era, and especially with the immense documentation of the period. Although it should be impossible to conceive of students of international relations worthy of the name who have not had some experience in and knowledge of the documents and monographic literature of the interwar years, unfortunately this is not always the case. This work is designed to alleviate this situation, for a student of international relations should know about this period not only to test and develop new theories but also to grasp the nature of change in international relations. Obviously, the interwar years are only one piece of reality, but knowledge of them will enable the political scientist to know the differences between this period and other periods as well as their similarities. It is to be hoped that, as a result, his generalizations will become more complex and more judicious and that some will even be scrapped. If this study does nothing else than stimulate the student of international relations to ask, "What can I learn about my subject from these years?" it will have achieved its purpose.

Finally, this study attempts to pose a question about the balance of power; namely, what does its failure in the 1930's to prevent World War II tell the student of international relations about the nature of the balance of power? It is particularly concerned with the question: Could the balance of power system have prevented the war, and if so, why were its principles not used to do so? This question leads to another: Does the history of this period suggest that the balance of power is no longer a viable instrument of policy? As is pointed out in Chapter One, there is a vast difference of opinion about the significance of the collapse of balance into World War II. One view of this collapse is that it was the inevitable result of a series of long-term trends that destroyed the whole basis of the balance of power system; another theory is that it was the result of a series of mistakes on the parts of those who were in charge of policy. The first approach is that of many political scientists; the second, that of Winston Churchill: but in fact both ideas are often held simultaneously. These views pose a further question: If the collapse of the balance was the result of error, what do the sources of this error tell us about the problems of making and operating a balance of power? The answers to such questions are important, not only because they tell something about the role of the balance of power in twentieth-century international relations, but also because they will shed light on the meaning of the phrase "balance of power." For the idea of the balance of power, like any other concept, must be derived from an interplay between abstract concept and fact, the one constantly informing the other. History is useless, or even in a very real sense nonexistent, without some degree of conceptualization of what is to be looked for; at the same time the true meaning and understanding of a concept can only come from a detailed knowledge of those events that are relevant to that concept. Without that knowledge of reality, the concept is worse than useless, it is positively dangerous; for only with an understanding of reality can there be sophistication. This study is an attempt to bring a concept of political science and its history together in order to provide some degree of sophistication.

It should be made plain at the beginning that the object of this study is not to show that the balance of power system is "adequate" or "inadequate." Rather it is to come to some conclusions about the specific weaknesses of the system so that lessons can be drawn and something learned about what should be done to correct them. If it is to be a useful tool of both politics and political analyses, balance of power must be considered in terms of the specific problems it presents rather than in terms of generalizations that lead to outright rejection or acceptance. Rather than reject or accept the system as a whole, it is necessary to find out as precisely as possible in what particular areas it is weak. A study of the balance in the interwar years will show, not that the balance of power system "works" or does not "work," but in what particular ways it can be used or how statesmen fail to use it. This knowledge may make it possible to say, *not* that the system should be rejected because it failed, but what the failure demonstrates should be done to make it perform.

To bring history and political science together is not easy. Having taught an introductory college course in international relations for over fifteen years, the author has long had a sense of the void that exists between the two fields. Conceptualization is necessary to give meaning to history, but the theories of international relations do not fit easily, and sometimes not at all, into the multitudinous variety and reality of history. History imposes its own will, so to speak; the chronological telling of a story asserts its own meaning. It is the duty of the political scientist to break into that story, to pose questions, and to organize its variety so that answers are provided. But such is also the duty of the historian. Yet though they may be seeking the answers to different questions, it is perhaps on this common ground of interrogating the facts of history that they can meet.

In a work of this kind the dimensions of the subject make it necessary to assume that the reader has a knowledge of the fundamental facts and trends of the interwar years, such as any first-rate textbook provides. Thus, for example, no attempt will be made here to describe the Munich crisis as such; instead, there will be an analysis of what that crisis means for an understanding of the balance of power. But even though this book is not a history of the period, I have not hesitated to plunge into the somewhat complicated flow of history at certain crucial points of the investigation, for there is where the stuff of international relations will be found. This highly selective approach means that many significant developments must be left out of account if they do not impinge directly on an analysis of the workings of the balance of power. As a result, attention has been focused as much as possible on the crucial relationships between Britain, France, and Germany; Italy and the Soviet Union enter in only, so to speak, as accessories after the fact. A narrowing of the field of discussion in this way is one of the problems that arises when political science and history are brought together. This study also assumes that the student has some understanding of the basic concepts of the field of international relations and, particularly, of the balance of power.

A word should be added about the organization of this study. The first chapter is a general and discursive consideration of some of the features of the interwar years as they relate to the question of the balance of power. The main purpose of this chapter is to indicate the various facets of the period that can be of interest and significance to the political scientist and the student of international relations. The second chapter deals with the Locarno Treaties and the establishment of a balance of power through the negotiations that produced those Treaties. The concept of the "broker" as a crucial part of the balance is here introduced and defined. The third chapter considers the period between Hitler's rise to power and the outbreak of the war and deals with the changes in the distribution of power within those years, the essential nature of Hitler's foreign policy, and the efforts of the French and British to maintain the balance of power. The emphasis is on the problems that a particular type of state, the Hitlerian state, can create for those who would maintain the principle of the balance of power. A final chapter attempts to answer briefly some of the more general problems put forward in the first chapter.

Many persons have aided the author in the writing of this book. Professor Hubert Gibbs, Chairman of the Department of Government at Boston University, read the manuscript at various stages and made many essential and penetrating suggestions for improvement and for overcoming certain serious intellectual problems that the topic presents; he also provided the academic opportunity for the writing of this work. But he has been performing these tasks for me for so many years that this is a suitable time to gratefully acknowledge the intellectual stimulation that he has given me as a friend, colleague, and chairman.

Professor John D. Montgomery, of Harvard University, and Professor Howard Zinn, of Boston University, read parts of the manuscript and gave valuable advice on the general approach to be taken. Dean Richard M. Millard, of the College of Liberal Arts, Boston University, generously arranged a sabbatical leave, during which the major part of the book was written. Professor Jack Walker, now of the University of Michigan, first encouraged me to start this project; the result is quite different from what he originally envisaged, but I trust that it meets with some of the goals he suggested. Professor Inis Claude, the editor of this series, gave a creative and useful critique of the manuscript, pointing out, specifically and concretely, the need for certain crucial changes and improvements. I should also like to acknowledge the support of my parents, who gave no criticism but simply offered encouragement. Finally, I must record my appreciation for the stimulus provided me by the students in my seminar on Diplomacy in the Interwar Years. In the process of talking out the subject they supplied many useful insights and opened up alternative explanations. The result was clarification for the author; I trust it was the same for them.

Miss Aurelie Dyer, who typed the whole manuscript, retyped many parts of it many times during and after her working hours with her usual speed and efficiency and, most importantly, with her own special brand of good humor and high spirits, thus easing the troubles of writing, rewriting, and again rewriting. Mrs. Helena Lothrop also came to my aid at a moment of crisis, typing during and after working hours when it was necessary to meet a deadline.

I owe a very special debt, of course, to my wife, Betty, and my daughter, Victoria. My wife greatly aided the writing of this book by unscrambling my scrambled sentences and by generally overseeing and overcoming the problems of style, rhetoric, and clarity. My daughter greatly aided me by her firm conviction, expressed at strategic moments when the interwar years seemed a bit overwhelming, that the book would be a "good" one. Together they provided the necessary infrastructure of affection without which the work would never have been finished.

I am, of course, responsible for any errors of fact or interpretation.

William J. Newman
Boston

Contents

The Balance
of Power
in the
Interwar Years

International Relations During the Interwar Years as a Problem in Political Science

The Outbreak of War and the Failure of the Balance

World War II seems inevitable as one looks back upon its origins from the distance of twenty-five years. Never, it seems, was a war more predestined by the march of events and by the aims of one man. Hitler was determined to have his war; Chamberlain was inept and naive. Ergo, World War II. There is a villain and a sinner; with two such characters, what else is needed to explain the outbreak of war in 1939, especially when the stage is filled with a motley collection of minor villains such as Mussolini and Stalin and minor sinners such as Daladier and Beck? If one ignores the roles of individual statesmen and concentrates on abstract concepts, such as the forces of history, the sense of inevitability grows even stronger. Then the war becomes the final act of a drama that begins with the rise of Germany after 1871 and the consequent com-

3

petition between Germany and Britain. It can also be traced to the Versailles Treaty, the disruption of Russia after the Revolution of 1917, the withdrawal of the United States into isolationism after 1919, to mention only a few of the obvious forces that made the war seemingly inevitable. Who, what, could have stopped the lengthening list of calamities that led to the horrors of 1939 and 1940 and the years that followed? History, no doubt, has a way of seeming to be inevitable as one looks back upon it; events seem fated to turn out as they did, and it is almost always impossible to show that they could have turned out differently. Once they happen, the reasons why they happened are too overwhelmingly impressive to argue about. But in this case the inevitability of history seems even more impressive than usual.

Yet, ironically, this sense of the inevitability of World War II is contradicted by the equally strong belief that the war should not have happened, that Hitler could have been "stopped," that appeasement was the wrong policy, and that a different and successful policy could have been adopted. Indeed, so strong is this feeling, that Neville Chamberlain has been made not only a symbol of the errors of the age but also its scapegoat. From this point of view, the war is the result of wrong choices made at certain crucial times. If different choices had been made, there would have been no war. Far from being inevitable, the war was the result of stupidity, false notions of national interests, and the inability to see what was obvious. If ever a statesman telegraphed his blows ahead of time, it was Hitler. Who could miss the message? Who could have failed to foresee what was required to stop him? It is because of the strong sense that World War II was not inevitable, but was the result of miscalculation, that it has become such an object lesson for the West, an object lesson in the terrible results and the mistaken ways of appeasement—surely the most dishonorable word in our political vocabulary today. It is because the word "appeasement" stands for the most complete error that can be made in politics that today literally no one can stand up and say he wishes to appease a state that is threatening another state. Thus, not only was the war not inevitable, it was not necessary in any sense of the word and could and should have been avoided. Sir Winston Churchill, in his usual shrewd way, has described World War II as "The Unnecessary War." [1] Needless to say, Churchill was not only a firm believer that the war was a result of mistakes in policy—mistakes that presumably would not have occurred had he been in office—but one of the prime originators and propagandists of the idea.

Such are the two diametrically opposed attitudes about the origins of the war, which are widespread even today. For the political scientist, however, the problem is not resolved in such simplistic terms. He must see the war not as the result of inevitability or of error but rather in terms of what it means for some of his basic assumptions and theories about the field of international relations. A study of the coming of World War II in the context of the interwar years may throw light upon one of these theories, the role of the balance of power as a stabilizing force. World War II poses a serious problem for the political scientist, for it raises the question of why the principles of the balance of power were not applied in such a way as to prevent this catastrophe. Obviously, if the balance of power was ever to be used to achieve a degree of stability, it should have been applied in the interwar period, for World War II was a catastrophe for all of Europe and especially for Britain, France, and Germany. Manifestly, a failure of titanic dimensions had occurred in the realm of the balance

[1] See Winston Churchill, *The Gathering Storm* (Boston, Mass., 1948), p. IV. "One day President Roosevelt told me that he was asking publicly for suggestions about what the war should be called. I said at once 'The Unnecessary War.' There never was a war more easy to stop. . . ." Note also Churchill's theme for this volume: "How the English-speaking peoples through their unwisdom, carelessness, and good nature allowed the wicked to rearm."

of power. The problem the political scientist must solve is why such a situation could have come about in the light of the idea that the balance of power is a set of principles designed to prevent such a total breakdown of international stability. Why did the states threatened by Germany fail to organize the coalition of forces that would have prevented German expansion?

According to any rational meaning of the balance of power theory, the war should have been prevented by the weight of the military and economic power that Britain and France, by themselves, but preferably in league with Russia and the United States, could have brought to bear on Germany. Even the most cursory consideration of Germany's situation in the interwar years will indicate the incredibly weak position from which she was attempting to operate after 1919. She had been disarmed by the Versailles Treaty and was faced by a large and powerful French army. Her geographical position between France and Russia still posed the same military problem as in the time of Bismarck and William II. Britain and the United States had control of the sea lanes and the resources of the world, while Russia possessed the immense advantage of a large withdrawal space. And finally, as recent studies have made clear, even in the 1930's the German Government was operating on an extremely narrow economic base, which was not even mobilized for total war until *after* 1941.[2] There is no question but that the balance of power *could* have been tilted decisively against Germany before 1939 as it was during World War II itself even after the Nazis had conquered all of Europe and large parts of Russia. Why, then, was it not used to prevent that war?

[2] See Burton H. Klein, *Germany's Economic Preparations for War* (Cambridge, Mass., 1959), and Alan S. Milward, *The German Economy at War* (London, 1965).

A Working Definition of the Balance of Power

In order to deal adequately with the problems and questions discussed in this study it is necessary, of course, to have clearly conceptualized the balance of power. Argument, discussion, and dispute about the meaning of the balance of power are staples of the study of international relations. Much effort has been put into this problem, and many different definitions have been formulated. The object of this study, however, is to develop a more sophisticated appreciation of how the balance of power functions in reality as distinct from the way it should function according to a heuristic and hypothetical model. Obviously, the way in which the balance functioned in the interwar years will not tell us how it functioned at other times, but an analysis of its workings in the interwar years will suggest some of the factors that must be considered when it is examined in other epochs. Because this study is concerned less with an abstract definition of the balance than with the way in which it appears in history—in nature, so to speak—a lengthy discussion of the problems and difficulties of defining it would be out of place.[3] Rather, for the purpose of this study, and in order to cut through the tangled undergrowth of arguments, a working definition will be used in this book.

This definition is composed of the following elements:

1. The balance of power has as its purpose the creation of a degree of order and stability in international relations in the absence of or without the resort to institutional means such as law, organizations, or even collective security or in situations in which institutional means have minimal impact and effect on the relations between states. Clearly, a balance of power can exist within an institutional

[3] For the best consideration of these problems the reader is directed to Inis Claude, *Power in International Relations* (New York, 1962), Part I.

framework; for example, within a university as well as within a United Nations. But the phrase "balance of power," as usually applied to international relations and as it will be used here, is taken to mean the operations of the balance of power in relationship to sovereign states and without the aid of formal institutions.

2. The balance of power is a system of relationships based on a given distribution of various kinds of power, such as military, economic, moral, and ideological.

3. That distribution of power makes possible some measure of restraint on the significant expansion of the major states that are a part of the system.

4. The balance of power restrains expansion by *either* an equilibrium of power between all the states or groups of states that are a part of the system *or* a preponderance of power on the part of one state or group of states. Either method of bringing about a balance has its own built-in defects. The first can become unstable because an equilibrium tempts a state to believe that it can upset the equilibrium in its favor by a small increment—an extra ounce —of power. The second can become unstable because the predominant state or group of states can either refuse to observe self-restraint or is believed by other states not to observe self-restraint. In this connection it should be made clear that a balance of power can exist where one state or group of states is predominant only if that state observes self-restraint. Such restraint is at least possible and in fact has occurred at various times in the history of international relations, but it is obvious that where a predominant state does not observe self-restraint, instead using its power to further goals of expansion, then a balance cannot be said to exist. We will see that Britain in the era of Locarno was a predominant power that for various reasons, some internal and some external, did observe self-restraint.

Several features of this definition should be noted. The first is that since the object of a balance of power is to restrain or control the expansion of a state or states, it follows that *any* distribution of power that accomplishes this end can legitimately be called a balance of power. Or, to put the same idea differently, a balance is seen to exist when a state that aims to expand fails to do so due to the actions of other states. The failure to expand in these circumstances is, in and of itself, a demonstration of the existence of a balance of power, and conversely, the successful expansion of a state against the wishes of other states indicates its absence. These conclusions derive from the fact that the whole purpose of the balance is to restrain expansion through the threat of countervailing power. If, therefore, a particular distribution of power achieves that particular objective, a balance can be said to exist. As we have seen, the balance of power does not use international organization, law, or moral persuasion to control power or create order, for, whatever the case in domestic politics, in international relations they do not exist to an effective degree. Instead, order can come from the fact that a state that hopes to expand will give way before an equal or greater power because of the costs of not doing so. However, this does not necessarily have to occur, and in the case of Hitler one of the crucial questions that must be asked is whether or not he would have given way if more power had been brought to bear on him, that is, could the principles of the balance of power have been effectively used against him?

Much of the agony over the definition of the balance of power comes from the mistaken objective of trying to prove that a particular distribution of power is necessary before a balance can be said to exist. But what actually happens is that statesmen are content to restrain an expanding state by whatever distribution of power is at hand. Obviously, there are degrees of manipulation: some balances may come about in "a fit of absence of mind"; others are very much the product of conscious premeditation. Obviously, too, other factors besides power can act to restrain an expanding state, as, for example, internal changes within that state. But if it is possible to show that the power of other states was the crucial determining factor, then an effective balance of power can be identified. Clearly, that is a big "if," for such an identification is not simple, due to the multiplicity of factors involved in international relations. Indeed, it is often very difficult to know until after the event whether a particular distribution of power will restrain an expanding state. This is one of the crucial problems of balance of power politics and makes the sleep of statesmen uneasy. Nevertheless, judgments can be made with greater or lesser assurance, as always, in international relations.

Not only can different types of power configurations create balances of power, but there are different means of arriving at these power configurations. The most obvious is to use countervailing force in its simplest and most brutal form to prevent or beat back the actions of a would-be expanding state. Such means are not uncommon in international relations and are the types of action most usually postulated under the concept of balance of power. But there are other methods by which a balance may be created or maintained. One of these is to use negotiation either to embody, fix, and manifest a given distribution of power that has the characteristics of a balance or to change it so that a balance is established. In this case the facts of power and the effects of negotiation interact, each modifying the other. For, however much the military situation is a factor in establishing a balance, the process of negotiation also plays a vitally significant role. Before the negotiations it may not be clear that a balance exists or whether the states that are a party to the balance consent to it. It is the object of the negotiations to make both the fact and the consent to a balance manifest, but in the process of doing so, the negotiations will probably modify the facts of power in order to arrive at consent. We will see these means used to strike a balance in the study of Locarno.

Still another means of arriving at a balance of power is to use countervailing power, not simply to coerce a potentially expanding state, but as a basis for offering concessions that will satisfy the state in question and hence produce a satisfaction that is general enough to make a balance. As we shall see, the extent to which concessions in combination with coercive power can bring about a balance varies depending on the type of potentially expanding state that is involved. But in general it may be said that the failure to make concessions may create such tensions that it may obviate the whole purpose of a balance of power and bring about the very instability it is designed to prevent. To conceive of a balance of power simply as coercive power meeting coercive power in a deadlock is not only to misunderstand the complexities of international relations but to envisage conflicts where none need exist or that might have been avoided. The judgment as to what concessions will lead to a balance is one of the most difficult to make in international relations and has been the downfall of many statesmen, and, yet, it remains true that the balance of power is not simply unremitting and unrelieved coercion.

The balance of power should not be confused with the condition of stability, which is a product of a successful balance. In order to achieve stability, the balance must provide some way of coping with the problem of change. Thus we come to the second feature of our working definition of the balance of power, which is that the balance is not to be identified with the status quo. For the balance of power to function effectively as an instrument of stability and order, it must provide for political, technological, economic, and other changes. It should provide for the possibility of creating a new balance if the old one has ceased to provide stability and order. Again, this is extremely treacherous ground for a statesman, for there are no simple criteria by which to judge whether or not a change is necessary or, if needed, what kind would be best. And, because the necessary changes can only be brought about by the consent of all the leading states of the system, the problem of preventing a particular balance from becoming synonymous with a particular distribution of power at any given moment is, to say the least, a difficult one. As we shall see, the weakness of a balance that did not provide for change was one of the main problems with which Chamberlain had to grapple in the 1930's.

As we have seen, in practice there are two forms that a *particular* balance may take; it can be either an equilibrium of power (equality of power) between the states of the system or a preponderance on the part of one state. The latter can refer to a holder of the balance, which causes a preponderance of power by throwing its weight on one side or the other (although a preponderance can exist in other ways). This third feature of our definition is of significance for the study of the interwar years, since it was British policy to establish such a preponderance by making Britain the holder of the balance. She achieved this objective at Locarno. In the Munich crisis of 1938 she continued to act as if she were the holder of the balance, although the substance of this role had been drained away. The shift in the nature of the balance is one of the crucial aspects of this period and poses the important problem of a lag in adjustment to the changing needs of the balance of power system on the part of one of the major states of the system. The most significant question raised by this problem is the role of the holder of the balance in creating the lag. A study of British foreign policy in the 1930's will throw considerable light on how the holder of the balance, precisely because she is the holder of the balance, can inhibit the changes that are necessary to keep the balance functioning and effective.

Finally, it is inherent in the definition of the balance of

power that the states that are a part of the system respond to each others' pressures and demands to some degree and hence make it possible for power and policy to influence their actions without destroying the system through a major war such as World War II. States put demands into the system, but also accept demands from it; somehow, modifications must be made at both ends so that a general, limited satisfaction results. This manipulation of both demands and response is the essence of the system. As we shall see, it was Hitler's refusal to play a role in the system established at Locarno that created the problem of the 1930's, namely, how to preserve the balance of power as a system.

Before Hitler, the balance of power as a system of demands and response had had a record of success in the nineteenth century as long as the balance was based on a preponderance of power with one state as the holder of the balance. The position of Britain in the nineteenth century as a holder of the balance made it possible for the system to function within the limits of relatively small wars, since Britain's weight on one side or the other in a conflict was decisive. However, this system functioned best in the first two thirds of the century, when other states were weak and poorly organized. Between 1815 and 1871 the United States was still in the process of internal unification; France was divided by a series of internal conflicts; Austria-Hungary was trying to cope with the problem of revolution and the rising tide of German nationalism; and Russia was too weak to effectively expand even into her immediate border areas. It was only in the crucial decade of 1860–1870 that Italy and Germany came into existence, the United States took a large step toward a new centralization of power under her old constitution, and France finally found a government that could give her a degree of internal strength and progress. Thus, within this extremely short span of time, essentially four new systems of state power came into being. British power became more and more restricted, and by 1914 Britain had lost her ability to play the role of the holder of the balance and to possess preponderance of power. In place of a balance of power system based on preponderance, therefore, a system based on equilibrium was established, with a consequent instability that eventually toppled the states of Europe into World War I.

The problem Britain and Europe faced after World War I was whether a balance based on a preponderance of power in the hands of a holder of the balance, namely Britain, could be established. The record of the Western state system in the years after 1871 did not augur well, but the fact that such a balance was actually established at Locarno in 1925, as we shall see, should give pause to generalization from what happened before 1914 as a source for the prediction of what must inevitably happen after 1919. The fact that the situation of 1919 was manifestly quite different from that of 1914 provided grounds for believing that such a balance could be reestablished. Germany had been reduced to a position of military impotence and economic weakness. The Soviet Union was convulsed in internal strife. Italy also was facing the problems of internal change. The United States had turned its back on direct intervention in Europe. As for Eastern Europe, the multiplicity of new states had created a regional system of international relations that in theory could be brought into the larger European balance in order to help restrain any German threat that might arise.

Not only was it possible for Britain to once again play her part as a holder of the balance and hence reestablish a balance of power system based on preponderance, but it was felt in Britain (and also, it should be added, in the United States) to be a vital necessity that this particular type of balance should be resurrected. The French idea of the balance was also based on a preponderance of power, but in this case with all the states of Europe lined up against Germany, and with Britain, most emphatically, on the French side. To the British, the French idea was a recipe for continual conflict and instability with a permanent coalition of powers constantly aimed at the throat of Germany. It was an expensive, quasi-war situation that would simply bring about another European conflict because Germany could only destroy the restraints that France would impose on her by military or violent means. When France and Germany came to a direct clash in the Ruhr in 1923, Britain was even more convinced of the correctness of her approach. What the British postulated was a balance of power system in which they, as holders of the balance, would be able to prevent a German attack on France, a French attack on Germany, and hence make it possible to safeguard France, prevent Germany from being forced to go to war to restore her position, and do all this without creating a permanent state of military tension. Since the French idea of a preponderance of power could not operate without British concurrence, the British were able to have their way in 1925. The story of this book is about the failure of this experiment and the failure of the British to recognize the obligations of a holder of the balance because of the inhibitions that the role of a holder puts on an effective performance of that role.

Analyzing the Failure of the Balance

There are four feasible answers to the question why the balance of power failed to prevent World War II. First, the principles of the balance of power may not have been understood properly or properly applied. If so, then it is legitimate and important to ask what were the errors that caused this failure of the balance and what do they mean for the concept of the balance itself. To understand this failure, it is necessary to consider the nature of internal politics in Britain and France in particular, traditional attitudes toward foreign policy, and the role of the individual leaders of the various countries who were making the crucial decisions. The 1930's were years of very personal diplomacy; Neville Chamberlain in Britain and Hitler and Mussolini in the Axis—each possessing the power of personal decision to a different degree. A study of the 1930's in particular makes it possible to evaluate the role of the individual as a source of the errors made in applying the balance of power. For example, did Chamberlain make mistakes? If so, how important were they? Why did he make them? Were they the result of his own views on diplomacy or were they the result of a frame of reference common to the particular culture of his nation and his era? It is a common assumption that the war came both because there were mistakes and because Chamberlain made most of the mistakes. Both assumptions should be examined by the political scientist because, if they are true, they raise a significant question about the balance, namely, if such incredibly expensive mistakes can be made, then, as a set of principles, the balance may leave something to be desired. In that case it is necessary to ask: Who is to blame for the errors which caused a malfunctioning in the balance? Those who failed to apply the principles of the balance? Or, because they are so vague, the principles themselves?

Such questions lead to the second possible interpretation of why an effective balance was not established. The principles of the balance may be inadequate to meet the really significant problems of aggression and expansion. The balance of power concept has been subject to many criticisms, and there are those who would reject the whole idea as a valid way of proceeding in the realm of international affairs. The Wilsonian critique that the balance must be replaced by collective security and the Morgenthau critique that the balance fails to resolve the problems of power conflict—the one from a liberal and the other from an exponent of the power thesis—both agree that the balance is inadequate. The particular failure of 1939 makes it possible to test these propositions and to consider in concrete terms whether the principles of the balance are really as inadequate as they are sometimes claimed to be, and if so in what concrete ways they are inadequate. All too often accusations against the balance of power and balance of power politics have been as inadequate as the balance is supposed to be, and have lacked specific content. Indeed, they have often been motivated more by ideological assumptions than by scientific procedure. Yet it is certainly true that the failure of 1939 raises the question of whether or not the principles of the balance are useful when the chips are down. Since the chips were down in an awesome way in the 1930's, we should be able to come to some conclusions about the usefulness of these principles.

The third possibility which must be investigated is that the specific historical circumstances of this period and especially of the 1930's made it impossible for the principles of the balance of power to be applied effectively. If this is true, one may quite properly wonder what kind of ideal conditions are required for the balance. Nevertheless, it is possible that the years to be considered here were a sport, a freak, constituting an exception in the history of the balance of power and making it inapplicable. Specifically, the argument would be that Hitler was such a special phenomenon that none of the normal rules of international relations would hold and that therefore none of the normal restraints of power or control could have prevented him from starting a world war. If such is the case, several conclusions can be drawn. The example of this period will tell something about the conditions in which the usual aspects of international relations, the normal rules of the subject, are, so to speak, in suspension. It will help identify other periods of history when the same situation has prevailed. It will make it possible to consider the years after the demise of Hitler in order to discover whether or not international relations show the same pattern of behavior; for if they do, the particular qualities of the 1930's can act as a guide to what has happened since, and if they do not, it is important to know that the qualities of the 1930's are not a guide. A consideration of these problems will make it possible to know at least some of the limits of the balance of power and to identify some of the traits of international relations that make the balance of power an ineffective system,

The final possible explanation for the failure is related to the idea of the inapplicability of the balance but deserves separate consideration. It is possible that the failure in the 1930's was a manifestation and climax of a long-term historical trend of decline and decay of the whole system of the balance. Such a possibility postulates that the outbreak of World War II was a part of a larger "event," which was the gradual erosion of the conditions that made the balance possible. World Wars I and II, from this point of view, become part of the same evolution and have basically similar causes. An investigation of the interwar years as a unit can provide some evidence to support or reject this approach. Was the collapse of the balance inherent in the whole system of international relations of these years and in the tensions and crises created by the Treaty of Versailles? Do the roots go back to the crisis of World War I itself with its explosion of the old political and social system of pre-1914 Europe? These general problems pose a more concrete question. Because the social structure of Europe changed in such a way as to produce totalitarianism and Hitlerism, does it follow that the balance of power could not have dealt with or contained the foreign policy objectives of a totalitarian state? The question is important because if it is true that the balance could not cope with the threat of totalitarian states, it becomes a dubious instrument for dealing with the international effects of far-reaching social and political changes within states and within a whole culture. Such political movements as Nazism are usually conceived to result from the breakdown of the basic elements of a whole civilization;

the efficacy of the balance of power as a means of dealing with such widespread and fundamental developments must be examined.

To deal with these possibilities, it is necessary to consider not only the 1930's, but also to analyze carefully the Locarno Treaties of 1925 in terms of the balance of power and to determine, first, whether they established a balance of power and, second, how firm and secure this balance was. Locarno has been blamed for many of the sins of the Hitler era. But such an attitude may lead to a distorted and incorrect view of what happened to the balance in the 1930's. It is quite possible that the causes for its collapse may be found in that period rather than in an earlier period. If this is true, we will be in a position to pinpoint the sources of this collapse with more accuracy than generalized statements allow and hence come to a closer approximation of what this particular failure can tell about the failure of balances in general. If the Locarno Treaties of 1925 established a viable balance, if, that is, the collapse of 1939 cannot be explained by the events of 1925, it will be possible to ask why the balance of 1925 was not or could not be perpetuated in the 1930's, to ask what changes occurred after 1930, and why the leaders were not able to establish a new balance that took these changes into account.

The Balance of Power in a Revolutionary Era

To bring into question the a priori judgment that the balance could not function properly because of the revolutionary nature of twentieth-century European political and social life is not to deny that the revolutionary changes that took place had an effect on the workings of the balance. Quite the contrary, the problem is to delineate those effects as precisely as possible. A consideration of the balance of power in the interwar years will make it feasible to analyze how the balance can be regulated in a time of revolutionary change. Indeed, the interwar years can be viewed as a laboratory in which it is possible to study and analyze the *usefulness* of the balance in an epoch characterized by revolutionary socioeconomic and political changes. Obviously, this was not the only revolutionary period in history, and other such periods, as the French Revolutionary and the Napoleonic era, could also be studied in the light of this question and a body of comparable conclusions established. However, the 1933–1939 period is of special relevance because of the immediate impact it has had both on the ways in which diplomacy actually operates and on the way we think about diplomacy. It is precisely the fact that these were revolutionary years that makes it possible to understand whether the balance is useful when states are faced with the task of creating international stability and order in an era of instability and disorder.

Because revolution occurred in the political as well as the social and economic spheres of European existence after 1919, the traditional "game" of balance of power politics became less traditional and more difficult to play. The consequences of this fact for those who had to make a balance function were to create new problems for which there was little experience to draw on in trying to meet them. One way of explaining the "mistakes" or "blunders" of Britain and France, especially in this period, is to realize that those who were running affairs were being forced to meet an entirely new set of problems that did not fit the accustomed patterns of international relations and for which there was no backlog of rules to use as a guide. Hitler was not, to put it mildly, something which came within the normal framework of experience of most diplomats and foreign ministers, even within Germany itself, where the foreign office (and much of the armed forces) was appalled by his maneuvers. Even the pre-Hitler years

posed problems of political and economic change that
forced the leaders of the states of Europe to face problems
for which they were not prepared and that called for im-
aginative responses they found difficult to make. To work
the balance after 1919 was to come up against a specific
set of problems for which there was no precedent.

Perhaps the most difficult problem that faced Britain,
France, and, it should be noted, even the United States
and Russia despite their peripheral positions, was correctly
estimating the dynamics of the foreign policy of Germany,
a state that potentially could overthrow the arrangements
of Versailles and strive to become a dominant power in
Europe. What, in fact, was the potential strength of Germany? Could she become a dominant state in Europe?
Would she strive to do so? What, in other words, was the
nature of the "German threat"? On what basis could one
make a judgment on these questions? On the basis of future
population growth combined with future economic potential, as the French were inclined to do? Or, on the basis
of an analysis of future German policy regardless of her
power potential, as the British were inclined to do? The
problem of estimating the power and the future policy of
other states has always been one of the most difficult problems of balance of power politics. In these years the problem acquired a new dimension because the entity which
was being considered—Germany—was in and of itself in
a condition of indefiniteness. The very boundaries of the
state were in question. The nature of the regime was in
question. The condition of the economy was in question.
The statesmen of other states were not dealing with an
entity that had solid content and firm outlines. Quite the
contrary, one of the crucial questions throughout all these
years was: What was Germany? Was she the Germany
whose boundaries were established by the Versailles Treaty?
Not many Germans would have agreed. Did Germany include the lands lost to Poland? Alsace-Lorraine? The Sudetenland? Austria? Was Germany a world power? a con-

tinental power? a regional (i.e., Eastern European) power? Or was she a state that lacked the prerequisites of power altogether, as the Treaty of Versailles plainly implied? Was she to be a royalist state? a democratic state? a socialist state? Everyone knew what Britain and France were, at least within certain well-defined limits. But what was Germany? Not only did her enemies disagree on the question, but Germans themselves disagreed. Needless to say, the very nature and direction of German foreign policy would depend on how the German leaders answered the question. Certain answers implied one type of foreign policy; other answers implied a drastically different type. The problem of estimating German intentions was compounded by the question of whether there was a German threat before 1933, and if so, what was its nature. Some Frenchmen saw the German threat as a constant, which was fundamentally the same during the Weimar Republic as under Hitler; the latter at least had the virtue of being honest about his intentions. Others, and especially many Englishmen, thought of the post-1933 Germany in terms of the 1920's, as a state trying to restore a lost position. We shall see that the difficulty of understanding the changes in Germany was responsible for a profoundly important time lag in the adjustment of the balance.

It was on the basis of these problems that Hitler rode to power, for he put forward a definition of Germany that seemed to resolve them. But the questions were posed before he came to power and had to be faced by even the best-meaning, most democratically inclined German. In these circumstances it was most difficult to make a projection about the future of German foreign policy, not only because traditional German foreign policy could no longer be used as a guide line for future expectations, but also because the Germans themselves could not establish a firm commitment in foreign policy until they knew what kind of Germany they wanted. Projections of German foreign policy based on economic phenomena, political traditions, or even the current situation within Germany could be at best only provisional estimates. It was for this reason that both Britain and France tried to influence the internal development of Germany in the 1920's through economic measures, such as the Dawes Plan, and diplomatic maneuvers, such as the Locarno Pact. The working of the balance of power, its theory, if one may speak of precepts as theory, assumes that the entities (or at least the major entities) that make up the system are relatively stable, that they are well defined, and that they persist over a relatively long period of time in the same fundamental form. As a result, it is possible to make intelligent and concrete formulations about how these entities will act under given circumstances. Obviously, reality seldom corresponds to its model, but in the interwar years the whole basis of the model was threatened. We shall see the ramifications of this problem throughout the whole period and not just in the Hitler years, but it is important to realize that this hurdle to the making of a balance is one that did not end in 1939 or 1945 but has continued, in one form or another, to disrupt the nice calculations of balance of power politics. It is, after all, difficult to know what the foreign policy of a state will be if one does not know what the state in question will be.

The difficulty of this problem was magnified by the second aspect of the revolutionary changes moving through Europe—a second obstacle to a proper functioning of the balance of power—the way in which the internal political life of states impinged on their foreign policy. This obstacle appeared in three forms. First, in all the states of Europe internal pressures, party divisions, and parliamentary conflicts played their usual role in helping to form foreign policy. In these years, however, the function of such forces was of special importance because there was no major state in Europe that was not involved in a serious class conflict threatening to weaken it in the face of other states. Consequently, it was more necessary than ever before to consider the internal situation of a state in determining its power and the role it would play in the balance. The incidence of this type of conflict varied from one state to another and for each individual state from one period of time to another. Further, other conflicts meshed with class conflict to produce especially explosive situations. The internal conflicts within Germany in the years 1919–1925 fall within this last category, since they involved not only class conflicts but also attitudes toward the problem of German nationality and power. And, obviously, the internal change which brought Hitler to power was of crucial importance to the whole structure of the balance of power. However, the impact of internal political systems on the balance of power should not be exaggerated. The statesmen who decided foreign policy were often relatively immune to the functioning of the domestic political systems and often in a position from which they could dominate it and impose their own concept of what policy should be. It is inaccurate to make generalizations to the effect that this was a period characterized by the dominant position of internal political systems over the foreign policy process. Yet it is true that the interrelationship of internal political systems and foreign policy was not only intimate but also different from what it had been when internal political systems possessed a greater degree of stability. What is important about this relationship is that those who were concerned with the making of foreign policy in general and with a balance in particular had to be constantly concerned with an estimate of how internal change would affect the balance. It was in part because Chamberlain and other British leaders failed to understand the nature of the change that had taken place within Germany that they failed to understand the nature of the change that had taken place in the realm of German foreign policy and hence what had happened to their particular concept of the balance of power. But, of course, even though such a statement is accurate, it does not necessarily follow that Hitler was immune to the workings of the balance of power because his motivations were solely those that came from the inner functioning of the Nazi state.

The second effect of the revolutions in the internal political systems of many European states was the fact that the traditional elite in the democracies, and especially Britain and France, had to deal with a new type of leadership in Germany, Italy, and the Soviet Union. This of course was especially significant in regard to Germany. One of the most difficult problems facing British and French leadership in the 1930's was finding out what Hitler was planning to do, or more exactly, discovering the relationship between what he *said* he was going to do, what he *could* do, and what he was *most likely* to do. This problem exists in any diplomatic situation, since there is always a gap between words and intentions, but in the case of Hitler the normal processes of diplomacy were disrupted by his personal and eccentric control over policymaking. Not even Hitler's own diplomats always knew what he was up to or what his ultimate goals were. It was, therefore, extremely difficult for those who were trying to formulate policy and to calculate the balance of power to arrive at a sound judgment as to how they should meet his next move. Information that usually could be gained through normal diplomatic channels was either missing or uncertain. To be sure, Hitler seemed to telegraph his moves beforehand and to lay down his program well in advance in *Mein Kampf*. But in fact these were simply statements of general intent and told his opponents nothing about the specific moves to which they would have to react in the concrete facts of daily maneuver. Indeed, it would have been a fatal error to take those statements as the ultimate and final truth of Hitler's policy because one would either have to "roll up the map of Europe" or prepare for a general war before there was clear proof that war was necessary. No statesman could have gone before the British or French Parliament in 1933 or 1936 or even 1938 and said: "Here is what

Hitler tells us in his book; gentlemen, we must declare war on Germany." Such simplistic reasoning was popular at the time and still is, but it is far removed from the reality of policy which was: How could the expansion of Germany be stopped? The use of Hitler's words—and they were many—as a guide to the general direction of his policy and his general aims could even be misleading unless they were put in the context of the specific political environment of those years. The British and French had to concern themselves with Hitler's specific moves, but to do so required more information from Hitler than he provided in *Mein Kampf*. Hitler's secret weapon, it might be said, was his ability to have secrets even from his own followers. One can go further; his ability to keep a secret was due in a large part to the fact that until very late in a particular maneuver he himself did not know what he was going to do. This type of leadership makes it exceedingly difficult, to say the least, to keep or establish a balance, since the ability to forecast is essential to the workings of a balance and only if a statesman possesses that ability is he in a position to apply those particular and concrete forms of power to particular and concrete situations that are necessary to keep a balance in working order. In considering the Munich crisis we will see the British, in particular, struggling with this difficulty—a difficulty so great that Chamberlain finally had to fly to Hitler himself in order to find out exactly what the man wanted. As Neville Henderson, the British Ambassador in Berlin, said in August 1938: "It is impossible to *know* anything for certain in a regime where all depends on the will of a single individual whom one does not see and whom few people see and who makes his own decisions." [4]

Equally important was the third problem created by the revolutionary nature of the internal political systems that existed in these years. The confused sense of national

[4] *Documents on British Foreign Policy, 1919–1939* (London, v.d.), 3d series, Vol. II, p. 112, n. 3. Hereafter cited as DBFP.

identity we have noted in Germany existed in Eastern
Europe, and was heightened many times by the large numbers of minorities that were to be found in most of the
states of Eastern Europe. As a result, the states of this area
were not only subject to disruption, but were forced to
adopt the most Machiavellian tactics to survive at all. They
were also extremely weak reeds to place in the path of
Germany, and they possessed few features that could lead
to any hope of their being anything but satellites (to use a
later word) of Germany, Hitler or no Hitler. Yet if Germany was not to become a dominant power in Europe,
these states would have to play their part in opposing her
expansion. Their weaknesses were, of course, not only
due to nationality conflicts; economically, they could hardly
stand alone, and the area as a whole was divided against
itself so deeply that every state lusted after a part of some
other state. The internal nationality divisions of these
states meant that they could hardly be called states at all.
Two of the most obvious examples were Austria and
Czechoslovakia. The former did not know whether it was
German or Austrian since the fateful year when it had
lost its position at the head of an empire, while the latter
was plagued by minority discontent that it was unable to
resolve before the crisis of 1938 occurred. In addition to
these confusions, class conflict and, in some states, a ruling
class paralyzed by fear of Communist Russia created a
situation in Eastern Europe that made it possible for
Nazism to bring these states down through penetration
rather than through outright attack. Hitler used this tech-
nique in both Austria and Czechoslovakia, not because the
menace of his armed forces was unimportant, but because
of the internal political systems of the two states and because Britain and France were not given the opportunity to
evaluate the changes which occurred in the balance of
power in the classical terms of one state attacking another.
By the time Britain in particular had awakened to the
nature of this specific problem—after Munich—Hitler

was already well established in Eastern Europe. But even if she had awakened to the problem earlier, it would have been a difficult one to meet in terms of the balance of power. The problem posed by weak and internally divided states, which are open to subversion from without and whose subversion by a major state can drastically change the balance of power, had its origins as a modern problem in these years, but did not cease with the end of Nazism.

Finally, the revolutionary changes of the 1930's brought about an ideological conflict within Western society that created a new environment for international relations. The breakdown of the Locarno balance in the 1930's was one aspect of the larger social changes that were occurring in almost all areas of Western life. The 1930's was an era in which fundamental and long-term developments became manifest and came into the open. Those changes, which reached their culminating point in these years, set off other changes that have formed the world in which we live today and that are still being worked out. For it was in the 1930's that the political, social, and economic systems that had come into being in nineteenth-century Europe reached their point of ultimate collapse and that new types of political, social, and economic systems were developed. These new systems were characterized by antidemocratic leadership parties, by mass rather than class society, and by statism rather than laissez-faire policies. However, these changes did not occur uniformly throughout the West. There was widespread and profound conflict over the issues presented by the new systems within as well as between the states of Europe in particular. Nazism and Fascism were not merely threats to the power of Britain and France (and the United States and the Soviet Union, too) in international affairs, but were also and more importantly threats to their whole system of values and modes of behavior. Indeed, it can be argued that it was precisely because Nazism and Fascism were ultimately conceived as threats to their values and way of life that they were seen as all-encompassing threats to the national power of these two states, since the power of a state is designed to defend a particular way of life—a particular society that is seen as distinct, unique, and valuable by those who are members of it—from those who would substitute a totally different type of social existence.

As a result of these changes, international relations in the 1930's was increasingly dominated by ideological conflict. The Nazis and Fascists, indeed, quite consciously brought ideology into the arena of international conflict and quite consciously tried to transform the traditional limited struggle for effective national power into an all-encompassing struggle over ideology. Britain and France were reluctant to accept this reading of international relations and for much of the decade refused to play by these rules. But as the horrors and meaning of totalitarianism in Germany and Italy became more and more apparent and less and less tolerable to even those who would make the most charitable excuses—and there were many such in Britain and France—the idea of international relations as a conflict between two ideologies became increasingly widespread. It was the coming of ideological politics that caused international relations to undergo basic changes in response to the other changes occurring in the rest of Western society. The course of international relations in this period was simply one facet of what was happening to a civilization as a whole and should be conceived as a part of a greater totality. As is generally true, changes within a civilization determined the real meaning and concrete nature of international relations.

In this sense it is not inaccurate to envisage international relations in the 1930's as one aspect of a civil war going on within Western society and including every aspect and all levels of that society. Seen in this way, the international conflict of the 1930's was qualitatively, so to speak, different from that of the Locarno years. Yet the new ideological conflict was not the only force operating on international relations in this period or even the single most important force. Of equal importance were the traditional concerns of power and of national interest. It is, indeed, precisely the interaction between ideology and power and ideology and national interest that is characteristic of these years, and it is the way in which the one affected the other that posed the overriding problem of balance-building in this era. Hitler as the leader of the Nazi movement and as the leader of the German state was not necessarily consistent; his decisions were characterized by a tension between his ideological urges and the problems of national power and national interest. He was able to use the one to reinforce the others, but the tensions remained even after 1940. Britain also increasingly felt this tension in these years; it was Winston Churchill's genius to make the fusion between the ideological conflict of Europe in the 1930's and the principles of the balance of power and to see—and show—how they were connected. But the injection of the ideological element into international relations confused both the British public and the policymakers until very late in the 1930's; they found it difficult to evaluate this phenomenon and to give it a place in their concept of how international relations worked. Hence, they tended to rely on the idea that the rationalities of limited power struggles were the determining factor in the foreign policies of all states. The civil war within Western society shattered the basic assumptions that had underlain the Locarno balance. The relationships between the states of Europe could no longer be based on the same set of judgments about power that were responsible for Locarno because a political movement of a unique ideological nature had taken control in Germany. Yet the British and French found it difficult to recognize this change or to understand what it meant.

This change in the context within which the relations between states were to be carried out posed crucial and unique questions which had to be answered in the 1930's.

Neither the answers nor even the questions themselves were obvious at that time. Never before had a prime minister of Great Britain been forced to ask himself what a political phenomenon such as the Nazi movement meant for international relations in general and the national interests of Britain in particular. It is not surprising that he gave some wrong answers. Obviously, he would have preferred to treat Nazism in the familiar terms of the international relations that had preceded 1933. But it was increasingly clear throughout the 1930's that it would be difficult to do so. Even Neville Chamberlain in his private correspondence described Hitler as "half mad," a "lunatic," and a "gangster." [5] But to describe Hitler as "half mad" does not advance the argument very far. The question Chamberlain had to answer was, "half mad" or not, what were the aims of Hitler's foreign policy and what was his power to achieve those aims? Was his foreign policy that which any powerful German leader would strive to carry out, or were there unique elements in his policies traceable to the peculiar nature of Nazism? To say that this was a period of revolutionary politics, of civil war within a whole society, may be useful, but a statesman must ask what this fact portends for foreign policy. The revolutionary quality of these years lies precisely in the fact that these questions had to be asked and that their answers were not clear.

Thus the long-term trends and the basic political, social, and economic changes that society was undergoing and that eventuated in the special qualities of the 1930's do not in and of themselves tell why the balance of power "failed to keep the peace." Rather, they pose the problem that the statesmen of those years had to face and the question of whether or not the balance could be used to "keep the peace" in such a revolutionary and unique situation. The particular qualities of the 1930's created the problems that

[5] See Keith Feiling, *The Life of Neville Chamberlain* (London, 1946), pp. 357, 360, 364. See also pp. 365–368 for other and different estimates of Hitler by Chamberlain.

had to be resolved if the balance of power was to succeed. They did not determine the success or failure of the efforts made to solve those problems. It is not possible to assume that the balance of power could not have been made to function adequately in these years any more than it is possible to assume that it could. The answer will not be found in the great sweep of long-term trends and changes but in the examination of the diplomatic efforts made to deal with those trends and changes. Yet this examination must also reckon with the possibility that basic and crucial changes had occurred in the conduct of international relations as a result of the revolutionary politics of the twentieth century—with the possibility that the 1930's in particular was a watershed in the course of international relations.

The 1930's as a Watershed: Munich as a Syndrome

One of the most significant aspects of the interwar period is the lack of unity it presents to the student of international relations and the profound gap that separates the diplomacy of the 1920's from that of the 1930's. Just as it is recognized that the decade of the 1930's was a turning point in the internal affairs of the West, so it may also be true that it was a turning point in international relations. But the problem this possibility presents is that of discovering in what sense a new kind of international relations appeared in the 1930's and the long-term significance of the change. For though it is possible to be relatively exact about the changes that occurred within the political systems of the different states in the 1930's and about what they mean—most Americans, for example, see the 1930's as a watershed that changed the nature of American life in some important particulars—can the same be said of international relations in this period? Did the 1930's bring about fundamental change in the nature of international relations that have persisted to our day?

To be sure, these years clearly represent something new in the history of international relations; never before, with the possible exception of the Napoleonic years, had the West faced that peculiar combination of power, expansionism, and dictatorship that Hitler embodied. Obviously, too, the 1930's were years in which the distribution of power between the states of the world was fundamentally changed; the decline of European power, the rise of the United States and the Soviet Union to their present position of dominance, the independence of the underdeveloped states all flow from the events of these years. In this sense the 1930's is one of the great epochs in history, one of those crucial periods that not only sums up decades of previous development but that changes the direction of political life and sets society on a new road and course of development. Such epochs are, simultaneously, a death and a birth. The imprint of their crisis is never wholly erased. The years of the French Revolution and Napoleon constituted such a period; the 1930's was another—and it is possible to argue that there were none in between to equal their impact.

At the same time, as we have seen, the nature of Nazism also makes it possible to view this period as a unique phenomenon bounded by the existence of Nazism. There has never been anything quite like Hitler and his foul gang, and because they so dominated the international relations of the era, it is at the very least feasible that when the loathsome creature was finally driven to ground in a Berlin bunker, a special experience was terminated once and for all.

Yet a recognition of the magnitude of these years does not tell whether or not *a new pattern of international relations,* a new way of operating and looking at international relations, was established. Were the international relations in the 1930's, despite the revolutionary changes of that

decade, a repetition of the fundamental ways in which
states had traditionally behaved toward each other or was
it a watershed that brought changes and innovations in
international behavior? The fact that new and startling
events happened in these years does not necessarily prove
that fundamental changes had occurred in the nature of
international relations. On the other hand, they should alert
us to consider whether or not a new era in international relations had opened. The problem posed by this era, therefore, is: Was the 1930's a watershed in the sense that in
these years new elements were added to the relationships
between states that have persisted into our own time and
fundamentally modified the nature of international relations? Naturally, one would expect continuity between the
conduct of nations from epoch to epoch. Yet, given this
continuity, it nevertheless is possible that something new
appeared in the field of international relations.

One view of the 1930's as a watershed has been so widely
accepted as true that it has become axiomatic and is one of
the most cherished beliefs of American and Western political life. What might be called the Munich Syndrome (stand-
ing for the 1930's as a whole era)[6] has become a model of
what should not be done and of a particular type of foreign
policy situation that is assumed to be true of international
relations since Hitler. Thus, the experience of the 1930's is
taken as a trustworthy guide to error. Situations such as
those of the 1930's will recur and have recurred since—not
to put too fine a point upon it—Communist states have replaced the threat of the Nazi state. The lesson of the 1930's
has become part of what John Kenneth Galbraith has called
"conventional wisdom." Political reputations have been
made by denouncing appeasement, for the model purports

[6] As will be seen in Chapter Three, the Munich conference and the
whole Sudeten crisis have been overemphasized as the turning point
in the diplomacy of the 1930's. In fact, it was the last act of the
drama; by the summer of 1938 British and French alternatives had
been so narrowed down that all that remained was to choose one of
two exit lines.

to show how an expanding ("aggressor") state can be restrained ("contained"). Manifestly, if it should be the key to the history of our time and to international security and stability, it would be of great importance. It is the conviction that the Munich Syndrome is the key to policy-making since the 1930's that accounts for the idea in our time that this concept is always at least potentially useful. The problem faced by Chamberlain at Munich is the problem we face, although presumably we will do a better job of solving it. But, whether we succeed or fail, a basic continuity exists between the 1930's and the years that followed.

The fundamental elements of the model are a negative precept and a description of the world of international relations. The negative precept states: Thou shalt not yield territory to a powerful dictatorship whose aims are infinite expansion. The reason for this precept is that the world of international relations is seen and described as a bipolar system of fundamentally opposed states in which one pole seeks to expand without limit and overwhelm the other. It is a world, in other words, in which the very balance of power is threatened with extinction because the expanding power will not accept the idea of balance, is determined to destroy the whole system, and will not accept the idea of restraint. Thus, the issue in this world of bipolar conflict is not essentially ideological, important though it may be, but the balance of power as such. Accordingly, the conflict is total, and hence the negative precept that no territory can be yielded. Anything allowed or given to it would not appease such a state but would only provide it with the means and the desire for further expansion, thereby destroying the defenses of those who would maintain the balance.

The model must be subjected to careful analysis in order to determine whether the ideas and assumptions on which it is based are valid and in accordance with the reality of the 1930's. If not, then the conclusions drawn from it and applied to the problems of our own time cannot be considered correct because they are based on a misreading of history. Correspondingly, the idea that Munich and the 1930's in general were a watershed would, in that case, be proven false, at least in the sense in which the model postulates a watershed.

The most important question to be raised about the model is the assumption it makes that Hitler could have been "stopped" through the application of force or a policy of "toughness" and that any aggressor can thereby be stopped. Is this assumption true? If it is false, the whole basis of the Munich Syndrome collapses, and the simple equation of force equaling, and hence stopping, force falls to the ground. If the equation is sound, however, it is necessary to show that it is true, to show what the nature of the force must be, and to show in what sense it would have stopped Hitler. Would military force have prevented the expansion of Hitler Germany? What kind of force would have been required? Were there methods that would have been essential to stopping Hitler other than those that could be grouped under the heading of military force? If Hitler had been stopped, would he have been overthrown? Would he have sought means other than military to attain his goals? The Munich Syndrome tends to hold within it the contradictory views of the origins of World War II described at the beginning of this chapter, namely, that it was both inevitable and the result of mistakes. Hitler is seen as a phenomenon of such elemental nature that he could only be stopped by the choice of policies that would have led to a major war, and yet he is also seen as someone who could have been controlled by the adoption of different policies, which would have stopped him without the necessity of war. If the latter is true, the problem then arises of how he could have been stopped, and when—in 1936? in 1938? The latter view also raises the question of whether stopping him was absolutely necessary to maintaining the particular balance of power established at Locarno. In this connection, it is important to realize that the basis of appeasement as it was practiced by Chamberlain was that the balance of 1925 could no longer be satisfactorily maintained thirteen years after Locarno. No one—not even the Czechs—saw the particular balance that existed in 1925 as sacrosanct, for even before Hitler took over Austria in March 1938 the Czechs were prepared, though most reluctantly, to recognize that Germany would be dominant in Eastern Europe. At the same time, no one—especially not Neville Chamberlain—was willing to see Hitler take over all of Europe and destroy the existence of the balance of power in Europe as a whole.

All of these problems make it necessary to be as clear as possible about the essential nature of Hitler's foreign policy in order to know what was unique about it and the type of policy it represents. For then it will be possible to understand the particular kind of problem Hitler's type of foreign policy supposedly presents to the balance of power and the specific kind of policy that is required if the balance is to be maintained. Consideration must, therefore, be given to the special quality of heedlessness and recklessness combined with shrewdness and watchful waiting that characterized Hitler's foreign policy maneuvers. His irrationality, which sometimes veered close to madness, made it possible—indeed, necessary—that he take actions that had no parallel in normal diplomatic situations and to which the classical idea of the balance of power found it difficult to adjust. How important was the peculiar quality of Hitler's diplomacy as a factor in the international relations of the 1930's? What were his objectives? Was he carrying out a plan of conquest or reacting to areas of weakness in Europe? Did he have a greater interest in some areas of Europe than in others? These questions are not as easy to answer as is usually assumed because of the irrational character of Hitler, but in dealing with them we will be in a position to come closer to understanding the problems of manipulating the balance in the face of such policies.

These questions indicate that the fundamental idea of the Munich Syndrome that "force" will "stop" an "aggressor" may well be a simplistic conclusion and that the whole problem of how to deal with an expanding state is more complex than conventional wisdom would have it. The Munich Syndrome is one interpretation of the balance, which emphasizes a particular aspect of the concept, namely, rigidity, as the means of achieving a balance because we live in a period characterized by the existence of states similar to that of Hitler Germany. It is this view of the balance that leads to the belief that the 1930's is a watershed in international relations. But since it is a view that grossly ignores the complexities of what happened in the 1930's, it is not a reliable guide to the meaning of those years for the study of international relations.

The Munich Syndrome is not only a misleading simplification of reality; it also is not a useful approach for the political scientist because it deals inadequately with the balance of power as a system. Instead of telling what the experience of the 1930's demonstrates about the weaknesses of the balance of power as a system, it focuses attention on the role of internal political forces and personalities as causal factors. Manifestly, these are of great significance, but it is also important to know about the processes by which states interact in a balance of power system and about the problems of making the system function.

A consideration of the balance in the interwar years as a system of interacting states rather than in terms of the Munich Syndrome offers a more useful understanding of these years as a watershed. Four aspects of the system changed during the 1930's in ways significant enough to warrant the use of the term "watershed" for the cumulative effects of these changes on the balance of power.

First, *the need to combine policies of coercion and appeasement*—if one may be allowed to neutralize this pejorative word—which had been the traditional need of a balance of power system, underwent considerable change. It was precisely Chamberlain's failure to grasp how the relative emphasis on these two aspects of policy had changed because of the nature of the foreign policy of Hitler that led to the greater failure of British foreign policy in these years. As we shall see, there is every reason to believe that the balance of power system could have restrained a Hitler. But it could only do so if the proportions of coercion and appeasement were different from that found in the policies of previous epochs. To attempt to apply the diplomacy of Locarno to Hitler was to misread a Hitler as a Stresemann. Hitler was a new kind of threat—he was a risktaker.

Second, given this threat, the proper combination of coercion and appeasement could work only if it was timed to come into operation before a state of equilibrium came into being. *The necessity for the proper timing for the application of counterweights against an expanding state* was quite different in the situation of the 1930's from that which had previously obtained. For, in this case, equilibrium would act as a positive opportunity for a Hitler to act, as we shall see. Thus, a preponderance of power had to be used to bring the balance of power into active operation at a time when the would-be expanding state possessed almost no power, when it was clearly and decisively in a state of inferiority, and when its transgressions were minimal. Such a need means that the actions of the balance system must be much more sensitive and precise than before 1933. Waiting was a luxury that could no longer be allowed.

Third, the diplomacy of the 1930's indicates that the *role of the holder of the balance* had changed in that the holder could no longer use his tacit power as an overseer of the balance but must come down on one side of the balance— clearly, unmistakably, and without dallying. His ability to manipulate the balance and still remain its holder was greatly restricted in these years. In this situation, where the preponderance of power is in the hands of a holder of the balance, he must make his power felt rather than act simply to maintain his position.

Fourth, and most important, all of these needs raised the problem of how to prevent them singly or in combination from creating such rigidities in the balance that no change could take place in international relations and that the system became a permanent state of war. Thus, Britain in particular had to face another need, that of maintaining or restoring the role of *the broker and the function of brokerage*. The special properties of this concept will be discussed and defined in Chapter Two. Here all that needs to be said is that the broker is a foreign minister or prime minister who carries the demands of his state to other states and their demands back again to his own state, and so back and forth until a tacit or explicit system of demands and responses on the part of all major states is achieved, which maintains or creates a balance. A balance cannot be maintained or created without this role and function, since a balance requires a system of response as well as demands, and there must be some means by which demands and response are brought together. Where there is no institutional means for this activity, the broker becomes especially important (though he would continue to play the role even if there were such institutional means). A balance cannot exist without all the states in the system recognizing the limits of their own ambitions because of the cost of not doing so; at the same time, there are certain demands they insist upon and that are recognized by other states. Since both demands and responses must be articulated to some degree, that is, made manifest so they are known to internal political systems as well as to diplomats, there must be an individual or individuals to convey the messages. These are the brokers. Since there must be some arrangement of demands so that a balance will come about, there must also be individuals to do the manipulating and arranging. Again, these are the brokers. The brokers thus arrange the demands and responses and make them manifest. Their role has to be maintained if the balance is not to collapse into a war without limit. That which more than anything else makes this period a watershed is the fact that the whole process of brokerage was under sustained attack in these years and had become increasingly difficult to maintain.

To understand both the need to maintain a process of brokerage and the nature of the problem which the diplomacy of the 1930's created for that process, it will be necessary to consider the Locarno Pact of 1925, in which a balance of power was established through a process of demands and responses—of brokerage—both to see what that process was and what was at issue in the 1930's. Locarno has disappeared into the mists of history, and is now usually referred to in slighting terms as "the illusion of Locarno" because it seemed to promise a peace that did not come. The widespread adoption of an antiappeasement stand and the Munich Syndrome after the outbreak of World War II has led to a rejection of Locarno as a symbol of weakness and naiveté. But, in fact, the Locarno negotiations were a highly successful result of negotiation between Britain, France, and Germany, in which the leaders of the three states played the role of broker successfully in bringing about a new balance of power. What happened at Locarno was a form of appeasement. But brokerage is not appeasement; rather, the latter may be described as one form that brokerage may take, a type of policy that brokerage, as a function, may embody and that a particular broker may attempt to carry out. A study of the relationship of brokerage to the balance of power at Locarno in 1925 and in the 1930's will make it possible to put the Munich Syndrome in its proper perspective by describing the problems of brokerage in these two widely different circumstances. It will show how the broker must combine coercion and appeasement to bring about a balance and how a failure to achieve the proper combination, and especially to achieve it at the proper moment in time, can destroy a balance.

It was the system of brokerage embodied in the balance of power established at Locarno that was at issue in the 1930's after Hitler came to power and that the British in particular were trying to maintain in their efforts to deal with him. They were trying to maintain it because their

purpose was to get Hitler to respond to the facts of power
and policy on the part of other states so that the balance
as a system could be continued and defended. For the
essence of Hitler's actions in foreign affairs—diplomacy is
hardly the word—and of the threat he posed to the balance
was that he would not respond to the demands of other
states and that he threatened to leave them with no alternative but defeat, total and complete, defeat that would
destroy the balance by a major, second world war. It was
this threat that the British tried to meet by converting—the
word must not be taken to imply a moral conversion—
Hitler to a system of brokerage, a system of not only making demands but also and at the same time accepting them.
To achieve that objective would certainly have required
the use of coercion by Britain and France at some point in
the 1930's if the balance of power was to be preserved as
a system and was not to collapse into war. But even though
the British used means and chose methods that were inadequate, they correctly saw that the problem was not simply
to defeat Hitler but to force him to admit the existence of
the demands of other states, to compel him to operate within
at least some of the limits set by those demands, and hence
to avoid the effects of the conflict that his total defeat must
entail. In this sense the need was not to destroy Hitler but
to change him, to prevent him from destroying the balance
as a system and thus make it function in new circumstances.
   The new question Hitler posed for the balance of
power—new, of course, in a relative sense, since sharp
breaks in history are more apparent than real—was how to
get the major state that refused to work within the postulates
and limits of the system to do so. Hitler's rejection of the
balance of power system did not mean it could not work,
but rather that unless he could be converted to a system of
brokerage, his rejection of the system would make it difficult for it to work and that the costs would be high.
Chamberlain tried to meet this problem by offering Hitler
a modified balance of power system that would meet many

of his demands and thus bring him into a system of broker-age, for in return he was to acknowledge the demands of Britain and France. The question facing Chamberlain, therefore, was not simply how to preserve *a* particular balance but how to preserve *the* balance of power system. Because he faced this problem, he was willing to modify a particular balance—the Locarno balance—in significant ways, but what he was not willing to do was to allow the principle of the balance of power system to be de-stroyed. The problem he and previous British leaders faced was discovering by what specific combination of coercion and appeasement Hitler could be brought to work within that system.

It was the existence of this problem and the experience of the British in trying to resolve it that makes this period a watershed and holds such importance for the student of international relations. Because Hitler was a polar extreme, the effort to convert him was difficult and dangerous; it required an exquisite sense of timing on the part of British policy and a delicate adjustment of coercive and appease-ment policies. There have probably been few states as diffi-cult to convert to brokerage as Hitler Germany, although even in this case the attempt had to be made and it could have worked. But although Hitler is an extreme type at one end of a continuum, he has, nevertheless, characteristics that another leader may exhibit to a greater or lesser degree. The failure to establish a system of brokerage after 1933 and the results of that failure were so devastating that ever since Hitler the possibility that another Hitlerian state or a state closely corresponding to it—one that would refuse to work within the principles of the balance of power system—has never ceased to haunt the West. It is the need to know how real that possibility is in any given situation and the nature of the problem posed by this type of state that makes it necessary for the political scientist to understand the diplomacy of the interwar years.

Chapter Two

Locarno and the Making of a Balance

I n the years between 1920 and 1925 the states of Europe were plunged into a situation of crisis and instability. The Versailles Treaty, rather than establishing conditions of peace, had triggered reactions that led to ever increasing tension and to the French virtually renewing the war against Germany by occupying the Ruhr in January 1923. The disastrous results of the occupation eventually led to the realization that some kind of revision of Versailles was necessary if stability and international order were to be achieved. Thus the Locarno Treaties were born. They were an attempt to resolve the crucial problems of Europe[1] in general and Franco-German relations in particular so that both French desires for security and German desires for revival would be satisfied. To achieve this aim it was necessary to change the entire distribution of power in Europe and to establish a system of restraint and order in the relations among its nations. The result was a balance—imperfect and incomplete, to be sure, as balances always are

[1] Since this study is concerned only with the balance of power in Europe, no consideration will be given to the larger balance of power in the world as a whole or to that in the Far East except insofar as these bear directly on the European balance.

— that promised the peace and stability Versailles had failed to provide.

In what sense can the arrangement of power established in 1925 be called a balance? By what process did this balance come into existence? To answer these questions it will be necessary to examine (1) the *series of events* of which Locarno was the culminating point; (2) the *power and influence* possessed by France, Britain, and Germany in these years; and (3) the impact of the *domestic politics* of these three countries on the formulation of foreign policy. This analysis will make it possible to study the role of the broker—represented by Austen Chamberlain, Aristide Briand, and Gustav Stresemann—in international relations, and will also lay the groundwork for understanding the problem of brokerage in the 1930's, when a different type of brokerage was necessary if the balance of power was to be maintained.

The Locarno Treaties

Before making an analysis of Locarno, a brief description of the treaties is in order. Technically, "Locarno" embodied a group of five related treaties, two treaties associated with it but not formally a part of the system, and a Note and a Protocol. Of the five related treaties, which were to enter into force when Germany became a member of the League of Nations, the Treaty of Mutual Guarantee (the so-called Rhineland Pact) was the most important. It provided for the maintenance of the status quo along the western borders of Germany. France, Germany, and Belgium pledged that they would not resort to war against each other except in cases of legitimate defense or in pursuit of action sanctioned by the League of Nations. All disputes between these states were to be settled by arbitration. In case of attack by one of the signatories the victim could appeal to the council of the League and to other signatories, who would come promptly to its aid; in case of flagrant violation notification to the League was not necessary. This treaty was guaranteed by Britain and Italy. The other four treaties, signed separately between Germany on the one hand and France, Belgium, Czechoslovakia, and Poland on the other, provided for the pacific settlement of disputes by diplomatic methods or arbitration. In the Czechoslovakian and Polish treaties Germany promised she would not try to rectify her borders with those states by warlike means. It should be noted that Germany specifically did not recognize the validity of the frontiers of these states.

The Protocol summed up the results of the Locarno Conference by stating that the five treaties were mutually interdependent and that it was hoped that a *detente morale* would result between the states involved. The statement about the mutual interdependence of the treaties was important to the French because it was a recognition by Germany that the sanctity of her borders was dependent upon Germany not using force to change her eastern borders. The Note was from Britain and France to Germany. They promised to interpret Article 16 of the League Covenant in such a way that it would be recognized that all members of the League should carry out the Covenant, and especially sanctions imposed by the League, only to an extent compatible with their military and geographical situations. The effect was to omit Germany from any participation in sanctions, if she wished, since she possessed a small army and was located in the middle of Europe. More exactly, it was generally understood that this Note would make it possible for Germany to avoid applying sanctions to Russia or allowing any power, for example, France, from using German territory for the transit of troops to fight Russia on the side of, say, Poland.

Two other treaties were signed at the conference. They were between France on the one hand and Poland and Czechoslovakia on the other. Although not a part of the Locarno Treaties, because Stresemann would not permit them to be officially recognized by the conference, and hence, by Germany, it was generally understood that they supplemented Locarno. They did so by providing that if the Locarno Treaties should fail to prevent attack, France or the other two states would seek the application of Article 16, or would furnish immediate aid if there was an unprovoked attack. Thus these two treaties were guarantees by France against a German attack on Czechoslovakia and Poland.

The Concatenation of Events

Politics, like any human activity, takes place in time, something the political scientist in his avid pursuit of abstractions sometimes overlooks. A particular event is in part conditioned by what preceded it, for what occurred earlier limits and partially determines the choices that are to be made. Contrariwise, what precedes an event makes possible certain choices. For while the next event in a series cannot be predicted simply on the basis of those that preceded it, they are, nevertheless, essential to understanding what happened and why. Thus, for example, Locarno would not have been possible without the Dawes Plan, the Dawes Plan without the occupation of the Ruhr, and so on, in infinite regress. Indeed, those who made Locarno had both the Dawes Plan and the occupation of the Ruhr as well as other events very much in mind if for no other reason than that most of them had participated in those events. Similarly, the student of Locarno must have them much in mind.

However, the conceptual apparatus of the political scientist must also be used. Because Locarno required the Dawes Plan as a preliminary step, it does not follow that Locarno had to take the form it did or had to come into existence at all once the Dawes Plan succeeded. The political scientist must look outside the concatenation of events for an explanation of the peculiar qualities of Locarno by seeking to understand how these events were related to the facts of national power, definitions of national interest, and the play of domestic politics. How did these factors affect the workings of events? And contrariwise, how did the workings of events affect the impact and nature of those three factors? It is within this tissue of events and factors that the political scientist must work in order to explain *both* the links between events *and* the creation of new events. Because it is not possible to predict an event on the basis of what occurred previously, it is necessary to deal with the question of how and why something new was brought to the time series. This involvement with the invention of new events within a time sequence is the ultimate justification for the development of abstract categories and theories by the political scientist.

The series of events resulting in Locarno emerged from the unresolved problem that dominated international relations throughout the years 1919–1925, namely, the problem of satisfying French demands for military security and economic reparations. France had failed in 1919 at the Paris Peace Conference to detach the Rhineland from Germany, as Marshal Foch had wanted;[2] instead, she had been forced to accept only a fifteen-year occupation with evacuation in three stages (1925, 1930, 1935). She had also failed to receive the security promised by the Anglo-American guarantee pact when the United States rejected this commitment. Hence, her continuing concern over the potential threat of Germany.

France tried to strengthen her hold over Germany by negotiating an Anglo-French pact to take the place of the Anglo-American guarantee pact. Since France was vitally interested in establishing a barrier to the East by maintaining the independence of the new states of that area, especially Poland and Czechoslovakia, she wanted Britain to

[2] See J. C. King, *Foch versus Clemenceau: France and German Dismemberment, 1918–1919* (Cambridge, Mass., 1960), *passim*.

make a commitment to Eastern Europe as well as to the borders of France herself. For only if France could prevent German expansion eastward, it was reasoned in Paris, could German expansion westward also be prevented. But the British refused to do more than promise to come to the aid of France if German troops attacked her directly. The breakdown of the negotiations in July 1922 led the French to make further efforts to achieve a British commitment to Europe by involving Britain in a more general system of obligations through the League of Nations.

The Draft Treaty of Mutual Assistance put before the League in 1923 provided that the members of the League furnish whatever aid the League of Nations Council requested for any victim of attack. When this provision was not adopted, the Geneva Protocol for the Pacific Settlement of Disputes was brought forward in 1924. It provided that arbitration procedures be established by the League and that any state that repudiated them be automatically considered an aggressor. The latter proposal was weaker than the former, but Britain rejected both because they forced on her the very commitment France was aiming at—a commitment to defend not only France but the peace settlement as a whole and especially the borders of Eastern Europe.

While France was failing to achieve her security demands, she was also failing to achieve her reparations demands. The French had insisted that the total reparations bill be set at the colossal figure of $31.5 billion. The British soon recognized that this figure was unrealistic and that if France exacted the last tithe owed to her, as she showed every intention of doing, there would be an economic collapse in Germany and in the whole system of international trade on which Britain depended. When the Germans began asking for moratoria on payments, Britain and France split apart; Britain was willing to grant a moratorium but France asked for productive guarantees, such as factories and mines, as security for Germany's promises to pay.

France unilaterally took those guarantees by marching into the Ruhr, January 1923.

The break between Britain and France was now complete, since the British refused to support France in the occupation of the Ruhr. Germany could no longer pay any reparations, since the German mark was worthless and she had adopted a policy of passive resistance in order to make the occupation expensive to France. The ensuing deadlock was broken by the Dawes Plan,[3] which was not only an ingenious economic resolution of the reparations question, but a political act of the greatest importance. It allowed France to back out gracefully from a situation that had led to her isolation and to estrangement from Britain. Thus, as a result of the Dawes settlement of the reparations issue, France agreed to evacuate the Ruhr by August 16, 1925. The Dawes Plan also made possible the economic recovery of Germany, and hence, the revival of German power. It brought Germany back to the "family of nations," or, to be more exact, gave her bargaining power, since her sovereignty could no longer be attacked by France as in 1923 without the assent of those who agreed to the plan. Because German sovereignty was affirmed in the face of France, Germany achieved a measure of equality with France. Now Germany had rights too, which were guarded over by the Dawes Plan and those who executed it, as well as by the British as a friend in court. Finally, and most important, the plan was a public acknowledgment by France that she would not and could not act independently against Germany, but must have an ally against her. French dependence on Britain was sealed at a London Conference (July 16–August 16, 1924), which accepted the Dawes

[3] The Dawes Plan provided for a system of phased reparations payments without any commitment as to the final sum owed. These payments were to be made in such a way that they would be related to the general economic conditions of Germany, who would accept some degree of Allied supervision over her financial system. To make the system work, Germany received loans from other states, mainly the United States.

proposals. France had attempted to use the reparations issue unilaterally to deprive Germany of her control over her most significant source of strength, the Ruhr. She had failed because Britain had not supported her, and had thereby been forced to accept the Dawes Plan as the best bargain to be attained. The lesson was not forgotten. After 1923 France seldom took significant steps against Germany without British approval. The British point of view about reparations, and therefore about Germany, had prevailed.

Although the Dawes Plan prefigured Locarno, and although it would be more accurate to speak of Dawes and Locarno as two sides of the same coin, the Dawes Plan in itself did not resolve the security problem. If anything, it made it more intense precisely because it was now clear that France could no longer move unilaterally against Germany and that German power was about to experience a renaissance. If France had needed security against Germany before 1924, she needed it doubly after. It was also clear that Germany would now push for the complete restoration of her sovereignty by forcing the French completely out of the Rhineland. The evacuation of the Ruhr was only a first step for the German Foreign Minister Stresemann. To get the French voluntarily to evacuate the Rhine ahead of schedule would, however, be much more difficult to achieve since France was there by legal right while French occupation of the Ruhr had been avowedly an emergency measure to secure the delivery of reparations. This distinction was especially important because Britain drew a sharp line between the Ruhr and the Rhine and saw no reason to speed up the evacuation of the latter.

The problem of the evacuation of the Rhine became an active issue when the Inter-Allied Military Control Commission reported that Germany was not living up to its disarmament obligations as stated in the Versailles Treaty and when the Allied Conference of Ambassadors notified Germany on January 5, 1925 that the first Rhineland zone, which could have been evacuated five years after the signing of Versailles if Germany lived up to her obligations under Versailles, would not in fact be evacuated. (If the first zone had been evacuated on schedule, the evacuation would have taken place on January 10, 1925.) Needless to say, the Germans saw this as a continuation of France's "Ruhr policy" in a different guise. And needless to say, German self-pity was rampant.

At this point a confluence of the German desire to get France out of the Rhineland and the negotiations over security for France through the machinery of the League took place, for it was on March 12, 1925 that the British Foreign Secretary, Austen Chamberlain, in a speech at the League of Nations, rejected the Geneva Protocol and hence reopened the whole issue of French security. The stage was now set for what has been called "one of the most intricate and strenuous diplomatic tugs-of-war in modern history." [4]

Given the situation in early 1925, the idea of a Western security pact emerged as a resolution of both the security issue and the Ruhr-Rhine reparations issue. A security pact that guaranteed the present borders of the Rhine would not only give security to France against German attack but also build on the Dawes Plan and make it possible to achieve the next step in the restoration of full German sovereignty through the immediate evacuation of the first zone of the Rhine and hopefully the early evacuation of the remaining zones. Now that the economic problem had been "solved" by the Dawes Plan, the military problem could be "solved" by a Rhine pact. Hence, there would no longer be a need for a Rhine occupation. Such was the logic and the hope of Stresemann when he presented the idea of such a pact in a joint note to Britain and France in January 1925.

[4] J. Korbel, *Poland between East and West* (Princeton, 1963), p. 159.

The idea of a Western security pact had been lying around the corridors of the foreign ministries of Germany, Britain, and France since 1922, when the then German Chancellor, Cuno, had proposed this type of pact with the United States as the guarantor. Throughout the Dawes negotiations the idea kept coming up among the foreign ministers. But it was the Allied refusal to evacuate the first zone of the Rhine in January 1925 that triggered off Stresemann's actions and warned him that Anglo-French cooperation and understanding were being revived. It is worth mentioning that the Allied note to Germany, which informed her that there would be no evacuation of the Rhine, was dated January 5, 1925, and that Stresemann's first note to Britain proposing the Security Pact was dated January 20, 1925.

Negotiations on Locarno went forward during the summer of 1925, although, as we shall see below, not quickly or smoothly, since the French still hoped to bind the British more closely to them than the British wished. On September 1–5, 1925, a conference of jurists met to work out details. The Locarno Conference was held October 5–16, 1925. The treaties were signed in London, December 1, 1925. On November 8, 1925, Briand promised that the evacuation of the first zone of the Rhine would begin on December 1, 1925; the Allies, in notes on November 14 and 16, said that the disarmament problems that had hindered evacuation were now resolved and that the evacuation of the first zone of the Rhine would start December 1, 1925 and be finished in January 1926, as it was, in fact. (The Ruhr had been evacuated earlier, on July 31, 1925, as the result of the Dawes Plan.) In the remaining zones of the occupation certain concessions were made by the Allies in the administration of their duties and in regard to the impact of the occupation on the Rhinelanders. Locarno came into effect upon the election of Germany to the League of Nations on September 8, 1926; ratifications were exchanged between the seven Locarno powers at the League of Nations on September 14, 1926.

The Distribution of Power, 1919–1925

What was the relationship between these events and the power and influence of Britain, France, and Germany? The basic fact of the distribution of power in these years was the predominant position of France on the continent of Europe, due, in part, to the fact that Germany had not been asked to accept the *status quo ante* at Versailles but had been forced to give up not only her power over other states but even the power to defend herself from attack by France. Germany was demoted from a great to a secondary power by being stripped of valuable territory and having her army permanently restricted to 100,000 troops. But French power was also due to France's dominant position on the Rhine and to the barrier to the East she attempted to create through alliances of mutual assistance with Poland and Czechoslovakia and through good relations with the other states of Eastern Europe.[5] Her position on the Rhine enabled France to come to the aid of the Eastern states by launching an attack on Germany across the Rhine should the latter move eastward. It also made possible an attack on the Ruhr, as we have seen, the importance of which cannot be overemphasized. As one who should know, Adolf Hitler, said when speaking to his generals in November 1939:

We have an Achilles' heel: the Ruhr. The progress of the war depends on the possession of the Ruhr. If England and France push through Belgium and Holland into the Ruhr, we shall be in the greatest of danger. That could lead to a

[5] See P. S Wandycz, *France and Her Eastern Allies, 1919–1925: French-Czechoslovak-Polish Relations from the Paris Peace Conference to Locarno* (Minneapolis, 1962) for an outstanding consideration of this policy.

paralyzing of the German power of resistance. . . . If the French Army marches into Belgium in order to attack us, it will be too late for us.[6]

Yet there were grave weaknesses in the French position. France's economy did not possess a large enough industrial base to support hegemony on the continent and especially to underpin the economically weak states of Eastern Europe. Further, France was dependent to some considerable degree on the payment of reparations by Germany, a fact that gave Germany a significant amount of power over France by virtue of her ability to deny such payments. In addition, the barrier to the East was to a large extent a fiction because the states of Eastern Europe were internally divided and economically underdeveloped and because the area as a whole was so rent with conflict that it could not act as a unit. Finally, French power could give France dominance over Germany only if Britain and the United States did not support Germany against France.

Although Britain played a crucial role in continental affairs in these years, her power was limited by the fact that her land army after 1919 was even smaller than it had been in 1914.[7] Yet her sea power, in view of the weakness of the other states of Europe except for France, gave her a potential might to intervene on the continent that could be decisive in certain circumstances. For she could, if she wished, exert either land power through a re-creation of her army or economic pressure through the use of a blockade. But the weakness of Britain lay in the fact that this power was more theoretical than real. Her economy was in disarray and she was absorbed with internal political conflicts; she had world-wide commitments outside of Europe; and she lacked the will to exert her potential power activity on the continent of Europe—a fact of great importance in the making of Locarno.

[6] Quoted by B. H. Klein, *Germany's Economic Preparations for War* (Cambridge, Mass., 1959), pp. 174–175.
[7] J. Luvaas, *The Education of an Army* (Chicago, 1964), p. 331.

The rest of Western Europe was a desert of weakness. Germany had not only ceased to be a great power, she had virtually ceased to be a power at all until she was rescued by the Dawes Plan. Indeed, her downward slide in terms of power was unchecked until 1924, and by the end of 1923 Germany was in a far weaker condition than in 1919, when her armies had sustained military defeat. She still had her economic potential and a large and versatile population, but these were sources of power for the future, not for the years 1923–1925. Before use could be made of this potential a definition of German foreign policy and national interest that fitted the reality of her situation was required, a task accomplished by Stresemann at Locarno. Once that was done, German power could be revived, but until then, Germany was as powerless as a modern state can be.

The war had either left the established states of Western and Eastern Europe in a weakened condition or created new states that were mostly impotent and struggling with the problems of internal order. Italy was in the process of reorganization after the Fascist coup. Hungary and Austria were forbidden to have forces larger than 35,000 and 30,000 troops. Yugoslavia was struggling with the problems of integrating diverse populations. Rumania was grappling with the difficulty of integrating a large, newly acquired area. Of the new states of Eastern Europe only Czechoslovakia and Poland showed signs of possessing the characteristics of national power. The latter was building, under French tutelage, an army based on a relatively advanced economy. Poland had been born from the Polish-Soviet war and was probably the most potent military force in the area. Indeed, she could have posed a threat to Germany under certain conditions; skirmishes were, in fact, frequent on the Polish-German border in the 1920's. But Poland was weakened by a geographical position that gave her no natural barriers to invasion and left her squeezed between two states, both of which had lost large amounts of territory to Poland and possessed many times her power potential. Czechoslovakia also had an effective army and an advanced industrial base, which gave her the means of defending herself against any possible enemy in the area. Together, the states of Eastern Europe might have disposed of a significant amount of power, but for the fact that they were profoundly divided by intra-area quarrels. Thus, even the one significant attempt at organization, the Little Entente, was a negative instrument directed mainly against Hungary and Austria, and consequently, further divided the area.

Yet Eastern Europe was a crucial area, the control of which could determine the distribution of power in all of Europe. Its importance lay in part in its economic and population resources, and even more significantly, in part in the fact that this area determined the power of Germany, and hence, the distribution of power throughout Europe. If France and/or Britain should control Eastern Europe, Germany would be weak. If Germany should gain control, France would be weakened by a loss of power to Germany, although French control over the Rhine would continue to give France a strong offensive-defensive position. Thus, as early as 1925, Eastern Europe was vital in the conflict between France and Germany.

What of the power of the Soviet Union in Europe in general and in Eastern Europe in particular? This question was still theoretical in the years 1923–1925 because the Soviet Union had not yet emerged from the internal turmoil and weakness caused by the Revolution.[8] That Soviet armies could act offensively and effectively was proven in the Polish-Soviet war, when the Soviet Union drove to the gates of Warsaw. That these armies were severely limited in their power was also proven by the fact that they were forced to accept a compromise settlement of the Polish border. Not only was the Soviet Union weakened by in-

[8] See J. Erickson, *The Soviet High Command: A Military-Political History, 1918–1941* (New York, 1962), Chs. I–VII.

ternal problems, she was also weakened by the existence of implacable enemies and—except for the Czechs—by a general fear of communism throughout the area. Even France, who might be thought to be on the lookout for friends, could not bring herself to ally with the Soviet Union in these years, and faced with a choice between Poland and the Soviet Union, chose Poland. Yet the potential strength of Russia was never quite forgotten by the French. Could it be called into existence again, as it was before World War I, to counterbalance the power of Germany? Was it realistic to hope that Eastern Europe could play that role in the place of the Soviet Union? Could Germany ever be contained without once again calling on Russian power? All of these problems would have to be faced by France in the 1930's, but in the years 1923–1925 they were still in the future. In these years Russia was not seriously considered as an ally by either France or Britain.

But she was seriously considered by Germany.[9] The Treaty of Rapallo, April 16, 1922, provided for a resumption of diplomatic relations between the two states and for the waiving of all German claims against the Soviet Union on behalf of German industries that had been nationalized; it also contained economic clauses that prevented Germany from joining international economic groups formed to deal with Russia. But, as E. H. Carr says: "The fact of signature was more important than the formal contents of the treaty. . . . The anger with which the Rapallo Treaty was received by the allies was a key to its importance."[10] For Russia, the Treaty of Rapallo provided a break in the isolation with which the West had surrounded her. Germany was likewise able to break out of isolation and even to threaten the West with close Soviet relations. Even before Rapallo the German *Reichswehr* and the Soviet army

[9] For an excellent survey of German-Soviet relations see E. H. Carr's *German-Soviet Relations between the Two World Wars, 1919–1939* (Baltimore, 1951).
[10] *Ibid.*, p. 64.

had initiated talks leading to agreements on mutual military aid.[11] German-Soviet trade also improved, the German share of Soviet trade rising from 25 percent in 1921 to 32.7 percent in 1922, putting Britain in second place.[12] Thus, both parties benefited on political, economic, and military fronts. Yet, because each state was weak, the power each drew from the other was limited. The military, economic, and diplomatic payoff of the treaty was slight in this period, the most significant result being a fear on the part of Britain, especially, that Germany might turn eastward in her orientation. Certainly, this fear played a part in stimulating British interest in tying Germany to the West through a policy of concessions.[13]

A word must be said about the power of the United States in these years, not only because the United States was the state with the most powerful resources at its command, but because she intervened decisively in the Ruhr crisis. American power rested almost entirely on America's economic role in Europe as the chief creditor of Britain and France, a creditor who insisted upon payment of the debts owed to her no matter what the cost. Since America disposed of enormous wealth at this time, she held a considerable degree of influence over Europe. This became evident in the Ruhr crisis, which the United States helped solve by offering dollars to Germany with which the Germans could pay their reparations to France and Britain, who then, in turn, used those dollars to pay their war debts to the United States—a somewhat eccentric system, but one that satisfied the canons of capitalism and had a beneficial effect on Germany, for it helped build and revive German industry, and hence, German power. But this economic power of the United States was subject to two strict limitations. First, it was used only in pursuit of financial orthodoxy rather than for political objectives.

[11] *Ibid.*, pp. 55–61.
[12] *Ibid.*, p. 55.
[13] We will see below that German policymakers themselves were torn between an eastward and westward orientation.

The American definition of national interest in Europe at this time was almost exclusively apolitical. The latent political power that American wealth represented was, therefore, never mobilized for use in foreign policy to the extent possible. Second, this wealth was precarious. In 1929 it vanished, and American isolation deepened. Thus, American power in Europe in the years 1923–1925 was spasmodic, restricted, and—to some extent—accidental and unpredictable. Certainly, the influence of the United States upon the events of these years was not commensurate with her potential power.

What does the distribution of national power in these years tell about the making of Locarno? As we have already seen, and will see in more detail below, national power, so-called, or crude power divorced from intent, policy, or concepts of national interest, does not reveal much about the way international events occur or about how and why a balance comes into existence.[14] But it does give some clues about the nature of the Locarno Treaties.

On the surface Locarno presents a puzzle because it established a situation that gave Germany greater power and influence than previously. It therefore brought about a relative decline in French power. Given French hegemony and the tremendous gulf between French and German power—military, economic, and diplomatic—how could such a decline come about? As we shall see, this was in part a result of the way France defined her national interest. But in part it was because there were significant limits on French power despite the discrepancy between French and German power. Some of these limits emerged in the fiasco of the Ruhr occupation; economic weakness and a consequent difficulty in carrying the financial burden of the occupation was the crucial limit.

But in addition, France's attempts to use her power to

[14] See S. B. Jones, "The Power Inventory and National Strategy," in J. N. Rosenau, ed., *International Politics and Foreign Policy: A Reader in Research and Theory* (Glencoe, Ill., 1961).

extend her hegemony beyond the boundaries set by the Versailles Treaty brought about a shift of British and American power to the side of Germany. France was extremely powerful in regard to Germany, and especially the vital Rhine-Ruhr complex. But France's power beyond a certain point could be exercised only with the consent of her former allies or against them. To be sure, France forced Germany to give up passive resistance unconditionally, and by the end of 1924 coerced Germany into making deliveries of reparations. But with the occupation of the Ruhr, the French-German conflict ceased to be one between France and Germany and became one between France, Britain, and the United States as well. It was the weakness of French power against *these* two states that forced France to pause. For if Britain and America threw their weight on the German side, France's power would no longer provide her with the same domination in Europe and over Germany. This was the prime political fact with which France had to deal.

Undoubtedly, France could have expanded her power in these years if she had moved toward a further mobilization of her potential. But France did not choose to do so. Therefore, the occupation of the Ruhr demonstrated the limits of her then current mobilization of power and, hence, posed the question of how to deal with Germany within those limits. It was now necessary for France to redefine her policies and her national interest with this demonstrated limit in mind. But the Ruhr occupation also forced the other states of Europe, especially Britain and Germany, to redefine their policies and national interest in regard to each other as well as to France. How far did the British wish to go in support of Germany against France? How active a role did the British wish to play in Europe? If nothing were done to resolve Franco-German problems, manifestly Britain would be forced to intervene again in another "Ruhr" crisis. How could that be prevented? As for Germany, how could she make the best use of the failure of France in the Ruhr? What was her national interest in the light of that failure? Did the failure of France in the Ruhr and the Dawes Plan open up a possibility of a new definition of national interest for Germany, one that went on beyond mere survival and gave hope for a revival of German power? The events and distribution of power in the years 1919–1925 posed more questions than were answered. Only if the states of Europe redefined their foreign policies and national interest in the light of events and the facts of power would it be possible to know whether a balance of power had emerged.

But definitions of foreign policy and national interests do not take place in a vacuum. Instead they take place in the context of an interplay between domestic political systems and the international system. It is the function of the broker to conduct and manipulate this interplay and, indeed, set it into motion. To understand how the broker operates as an agent of *both* systems it will be necessary to understand the domestic framework within which Chamberlain, Briand, and Stresemann had to work and the demands these domestic systems made on them. We will then be able to make an analysis of how the three brokers of the Locarno balance, Chamberlain, Briand, and Stresemann, played their role.

Domestic Politics and the Definition of National Interests

The domestic concerns and internal political systems of France, Britain, and Germany were clearly of crucial importance in forming the concepts of national interests that made Locarno possible. By 1925 the political parties and public opinion of each of the three states were willing to accept a resolution of the Franco-German conflict that would be based on concessions to Germany and German concessions to France. But the internal political systems of these three states did more than create a passive environment that was friendly to the Locarno idea. Rather, they were active agents in bringing about the Locarno Treaties and in creating the ideas of national interest that underlay them. The political systems of the three states were all making certain specific demands on those who represented their states in the international system. Locarno, therefore, can be seen as the outcome of what these systems wanted to achieve in the year 1925 and of the direction they wanted international affairs to take. The British desire for a "final" settlement of the Franco-German conflict, the French refusal to pay the costs of active antagonism toward Germany, and the German desire to free its western frontiers of the French presence came together in the year 1925 to produce definitions of national interest for the three states that pointed directly to the type of agreement made at Locarno.

Thus, it was in the domestic political systems of these states that the facts of national power and the concatenation of events were brought together to formulate specific concepts of national interest. Indeed, since individuals participate in international relations mainly through the internal political systems of independent and separate states, it could only be through the workings of these systems that conclusions about the national interest could be drawn from the facts of power and events. There was nothing "inherent" in either one or the other that necessarily led to Locarno. To be sure, in the case of all three states, the impact of the events of 1923–1925 made each state weigh the costs of alternative foreign policies in terms of the facts of power and confronted each of them with the problem of choosing between those alternatives. The internal political systems of the three states absorbed the implications of these events and reacted to them. But these events did not speak for themselves; they led to no predetermined conclusion and supplied no answer to the question of what the national interest should be. Instead, they simply posed problems and questions. To provide an answer, they had to be evaluated in terms of some kind of framework.

These events were evaluated not only in terms of national interest but also in terms of domestic political considerations; indeed, the two can hardly be separated in the process of thinking about foreign policy and national interest that went on in the three states at this time. In the debate about what should be done next in foreign policy, after the Ruhr occupation, the participants in each state had an image of the power they wanted their state to achieve and the position they wanted it to have vis-à-vis other states. Vague though these ideas of national interest might have been, they were the framework in which problems of foreign policy were considered. Yet, at the same time, certain domestic needs and the impact of foreign policy on those needs also were being considered. The idea of the national interest implies a concern for the domestic affairs of a nation as well as for its foreign affairs. Thus, the internal political systems of those states were considering the problem of the welfare of the nation as a whole and not just its foreign policy problems. As a result, there were certain foreign policy aims that were desirable, but which were rejected because of their high internal costs.

The ideas of national interest that emerged from the attempts of Britain, France, and Germany to define the needs of both foreign and domestic policy can be summarized as follows. In Britain, there was general agreement that her commitments on the continent of Europe should be severely limited so that attention could be focused on resuming the economic life of the nation without a heavy burden of armaments. Furthermore, Britain obviously had to consider other foreign interests—in the Empire, the Commonwealth, the Far East, and last but hardly least, in Ireland. Finally, the domestic political system of Britain was deeply engaged in dealing with the issues of class conflict that had emerged with the rise of the Labor Party as a powerful party and with the strikes that occurred as a result of the impact of the postwar economic situation on the British economy. For all of these reasons, the British were not willing to accept the implications of a stronger League of Nations through the Draft Treaty or the Geneva Protocol; the British political system would not have tolerated a closer tie with France or commitments to Eastern Europe. Its demand was for a minimum of commitment and a maximum of security in Europe—a demand which posed a nice problem for the British Government and the foreign secretary in particular.

The French political system was undergoing a similar evolution, ironic in view of France's obsession with the threat of Germany. Here, too, attention was being increasingly focused on the problems of economic reconstruction and the avoidance of higher taxes. Hence, the paradox of the demand placed on France's leaders by this system. It is well described by Pierre Renouvin: "The anxiety to assure the security of the country against German revenge without asking the people to make a prolonged military effort was the dominant preoccupation." [15] The shift to this preoccupation became especially marked when Poincaré was ejected from office to be followed by Herriot and Briand, leaders who were no less anti-German than Poincaré but who were supported by groups concerned with domestic problems as well. Poincaré had come to power on the back of the *chambre bleu* that was bent upon stringent controls on Germany. But by 1924 the turn of the wheel had brought other concerns to the front, and even Poincaré, if he had remained in power, would have found it impossible to maintain his rigid stand of 1923. The French were now seeking a way of liquidating the war without exposing themselves once again to the threat of Germany—another nice problem for a foreign minister to solve.

Within Germany the situation was even more confused.

[15] P. Renouvin, *Histoire des Relations Internationales*, Vol. 7, *Les Crises du xxᵉ Siècle: De 1914 à 1929* (Paris, 1957), p. 234.

The defeat of 1919 combined with the establishment of a new German state meant that a totally new definition of national interest must be created at the very time when deep internal divisions had come into being over the very nature of the German state. All Germans agreed, of course, on the proposition that Germany should restore her national power as fast as possible. But the crucial question, a question that would determine the fate of Europe as well as Germany, was how? Through cooperation with France or against France? The German right wing, and especially the German National People's Party (DNVP), essentially wanted to continue the war with France through a system of alliances with the Soviet Union and by refusing reparations to France. As a result, it rejected the whole Locarno idea and thus opened a profound split in Germany in which opposition to Locarno coincided with opposition to the Weimar Republic. It was this coincidence of opposition that gave Britain and France so much concern, for an internal shift of politics or even parties to the right in Germany would jeopardize the whole Locarno settlement and thus make its provisions a source of weakness to Britain and France. Thus, although the need to restart German industry after the Ruhr occupation forced the center parties, such as the German People's Party (DVP) and the Center Party, to cooperate with the Social Democrats in working out a *modus vivendi* with France, there was nevertheless a deep division in Germany over foreign policy. It was these dual and conflicting demands that the German foreign minister had to face and somehow resolve.

It is manifest that while the demands of the internal political systems of Britain, France, and Germany all pointed in the general direction of Locarno, there were also cross currents that presented immense problems to those in charge of foreign policy. The interpretations of events and the conclusions arrived at by the three political systems gave only the most general prescriptions for action. Although the process by which the systems digested the facts of international life clarified the situation to a degree, the demands they made were vague and even contradictory. For this reason, those who had to make concrete foreign policies not only faced difficult problems of reconciling various aspects of these demands, but also retained considerable discretion. Indeed, they retained so much discretion that they were forced to take over the process of policymaking where the internal political system left off.

It is because the domestic political systems can go only so far in resolving the issues of international relations that the concrete embodiment of the demands the domestic systems put to the international system takes place under the leadership of those individuals who are most intimately involved with *both* systems. Someone (or some group) has to take the lead in pointing out the issues, relaying information, postulating solutions, calculating the costs of various alternatives, and presenting these to the internal political system. Someone (or some group) has to present the demands of his internal political system to the other states composing the international system and to send back the demands made by those other states. If the internal political systems and the international political system are to come together, it is necessary that there be a broker (or group of brokers) who will carry information back and forth and who will also seek modifications in the position of each participant so that eventually a bargain can be struck. To see how the demands of the internal political systems of Britain, France, and Germany in 1925 were translated into a specific balance of power at Locarno it will be necessary to consider the brokerage process at Locarno. First, however, various aspects of the broker's role must be described.

Brokerage and the Locarno Treaties

In dealing with the creation of the Locarno Treaties the object will be to describe brokerage as a means of achieving a balance between Britain, France, and Germany and, therefore, to present a study of the way in which brokerage can successfully be used to create a balance of power. In an analysis of the relations between Britain, France, and Germany during the era of Hitler in the following chapter, the failure of brokerage to maintain the balance of power will be studied. Some of the essential features of brokerage, of the balance of power, and of the relationships between them will emerge from both studies.

Obviously, there is no such thing as a pure and unadulterated broker who is totally detached from the affairs of his state in international relations because those who carry out this function do so as members of their national community and have the interests of that community as they see them very much at heart. The broker need not, and probably will not, be "sympathetic" to the demands of other states or urge compromise. Quite the contrary, his function is to realize as many of the demands of his own internal political system as possible. Brokerage is one way of achieving those demands.

Brokerage is a method of linkage, of establishing communication, between a group of states that will lead to some kind of either *tacit* or *explicit* agreement about the distribution of power. It does this by modifying the demands of the internal political systems of the various states. As a result of these modifications, each state achieves some degree of freedom to pursue its objectives while recognizing limits on that freedom; hence, each state modifies its objectives in the light of the objectives of the other states. The alternative to such a process would be either a complete vacuum in the relationships between states or unlimited conflict.[16] Brokerage is the means of bringing together, making known, comparing, and changing the demands of the individual members of a group of states.

[16] Obviously, the many relationships that exist between one state and another may partake of all three alternatives at once in different spheres of activity.

Accordingly, each state knows what the reactions of the other states will be if it takes a certain action, what they will allow it to do, what they will not allow it to do, and the costs of acting contrary to the limits they have established. But in addition, and more importantly, each state sufficiently modifies its policy to at least attempt to come to some agreement on a distribution of power that will create both *opportunities and limits* for all the states participating in the process. It does this because the alternative is precisely either a vacuum in relationships or unlimited conflict. Obviously, the more explicit such an agreement can be, the more stable (other things being equal) it will be. Most agreements, however, are not explicit; they are tacit. Although one form of brokerage is that which takes place around a conference table, it is clear that it can occur even though there is no meeting or conference or formal negotiation or even formal contact. Instead, it can occur through a process of taking in and putting forth demands and modifying policies in the light of the results.

Brokerage is an essential aspect of the creation and maintenance of a balance of power. Without it there can be no balance, tacit or explicit, for there would be no way in which the demands each state in a balance makes on the other states can be at one and the same time both recognized by those other states and changed in the light of their reactions. Only through this process can there be established those limits on power that are the essence of a balance of power. Brokerage is the only means in international relations, where law and institutions are so weak, by which limits on power can be created; hence, it is the *sine qua non* of a balance. Thus, successful brokerage is the way in which a group of states recognizes and agrees upon the limits to their activities and thus makes a balance. It is the means by which the demands of the internal political systems are put into the international system and modified in the interests, not of domestic needs, but of international requirements for creating a balance.

The broker function must be carried out by those who are in close, constant, and intimate contact with the other states involved in a particular issue. Not many domestic politicians or leaders can play this role, for they lack the requisite knowledge, credentials, and specialization; they simply cannot know what the foreign offices know. At the same time, those who play this role must of necessity be of some importance in the domestic affairs of their nation, for otherwise they would not be in a position of influencing domestic politics on the issues in which they are involved. The broker must be able to stand up before his domestic public and on occasion tell it—even though discreetly— what it *cannot* have and what it must *postpone*. He must also be able to negotiate with domestic political forces and to convince them and the public that a particular bargain does in fact meet the definition of national interest, a definition that he probably helped form and that he now subtly re-forms so that it will fit the facts of what he thinks is feasible in the international system. He may also have to tell the public that there will be no bargain, that negotiations are broken off. To do all this, to be able to lead the internal political system, he must be an individual of considerable prestige at home and also a politician, someone who can sense the political climate, who knows what he can and cannot do in his dealings with other states, who can win approval at home for what he has done and assure those with whom he is negotiating that he can win that approval, a subject in which they are likely to have considerable interest. To perform this task adequately he must not only be an active practitioner of domestic politics, but someone who is involved in the formulation of the demands being made by his state. In practice he will be such an individual; indeed, he probably will have helped formulate those demands with an eye to the bargaining situation he foresaw when a particular issue first arose.

The broker is, thus, someone who stands between two political systems with a foot in each. The number of individuals who can do this is necessarily limited at any given moment of time. Indeed, in situations where power is dispersed within a state and no strong leadership available, there may be no one in a position to act as an effective broker; if this is so, then a state will be in an extremely weak position to negotiate. However, in most cases a broker is available. He will be either the Prime Minister (or other executive head) and/or the foreign minister. In some instances the two will work together; in other instances one or the other will be dominant. (And in some instances, too, there will be conflict between them.)

Brokerage is not, to say the least, a very pleasant or rewarding task; that is why it is so seldom recognized for what it is; no domestic politician in his right mind would ever admit to being a broker, since to do so would imply that he was not "sincere" in putting forth the demands of his state, that he was detached from his own system. Yet if this role is not effectively carried out, there is no contact between the domestic and international systems. The only way that contact can be made is for the broker to truly play his role of representing the demands of the other states. If he should fail to do this and do it accurately, his internal political system will formulate its demands in ignorance—a not unknown situation but one that is disastrous.[17]

Obviously, these qualifications mean that diplomats in the narrow sense of the term, ambassadors, foreign office functionaries, and so forth, seldom qualify as brokers although they may in fact play some slight role as brokers at

[17] It is obvious that the concept of the broker in international relations that is presented here is far different from that of the "honest broker" as that term is popularly used. The latter refers to someone who is not engaged in a particular conflict, who is from a quasi-neutral state, and who tries to bring two opposing sides together through a sort of mediation process. In the analysis given above, the broker is seen as fully engaged in the conflict situation as a participant in both domestic and international affairs.

various stages of a negotiation. Instead, such individuals function as a team under the direction of the broker and support his role—a position that can sometimes be of great significance in determining the way in which the broker operates, the positions he takes, and the information he possesses. Much of the information that comes to the internal political system and that is of vital importance in the process by which it formulates its demands comes from the broker, who in turn acquires it from the diplomats, who exercise a screening role of great significance. By the judicious selection of facts to be released to the internal political system these individuals, under the direction of the broker, may almost predetermine in certain cases what the response of the internal political situation will be to a particular issue. Indeed, they may select the facts that they will reveal to the broker himself and thus help predetermine his reactions; this is, however, more difficult because the broker usually has his own knowledge and independent sources as a check on the activities of his team.

The existence of a group of brokers from different states is a concrete embodiment of the international system. It is in the relationships between these brokers that one can observe the international system in operation. The international system may, of course, be defined as a group of states interacting with each other in a given period of time over a particular issue or set of issues. But the crucial point at which states interact, although not the only one, is that point where the brokers are at work, each presenting the demands of his internal political system and trying to achieve these demands through a process of bargaining. Sometimes there will be no bargain struck; the antagonisms between the states and the conflict between the demands of the internal political systems will be too great and the brokers will not be able to bring about agreement. Sometimes the brokers will deliberately refuse to play their role and hence bring about stalemate. The broker is not a

magician; he can operate only within certain closely defined limits to modify demands and make a bargain. But
even where there is an antagonistic relationship, the broker
will still function as he strives to make the best deal possible
for his state; indeed, since there is always a degree of
antagonism in the international system, this is the normal
mode of operation for the broker. To achieve this bargain
in an antagonistic situation, however, the broker does not
merely present the demands of his state or seek to make the
best possible deal for his state; such an activity would not
distinguish him as a broker. What identifies his role is the
fact that he is also a member of the international system
*and that in a situation of antagonism he also represents
that system at home.*

As a representative of both the domestic and international political systems, the broker may choose to or feel
forced to emphasize certain aspects of his nation's demands
and to redefine them in certain ways. Indeed, because the
demands of an internal political system are bound to be
gross in nature, and sometimes vague and even contradictory, as we have seen in the case of Britain, France, and
Germany, it is his duty to modify them in such a way that
they will be most useful. Contrariwise, he will also find it
necessary to stress and emphasize certain aspects of the
demands of other states on his state and to modify them so
that they will create the effect he wishes in his own state.
Thus, because he is, as broker, the individual most intimately connected with the international system, and because he is the key link between it and his own state, he
can in certain circumstances dominate the situation within
his state and direct it to the end of making those demands
he thinks most appropriate. Many factors are responsible,
of course, for the degree of discretion possessed by a
specific broker. One, however, may be singled out as being
of special importance. The extent to which the domestic
political system accepts the idea of foreign policy operating

in the context of a larger international system rather than in terms of the single objective of a particular foreign policy can determine whether or not the brokerage role will be stultified. We shall see the effects of this approach to national interest when we consider Hitler's foreign policy in the next chapter.

It is difficult to overrate the importance of the broker. He is as crucial a factor in international relations as are the elements of power, ideas of the national interest, or the internal political system, for he is the point at which all these intersect. He is the agency through which they become real and concrete entities. In the process of making them real and concrete he necessarily plays a major part in determining what they mean in reality.

Having considered an abstract description of brokerage, it will now be possible to give more specific content and meaning to the concept through a study of an actual process of brokerage.

The Origins of Locarno: The Role of the Three Brokers

The security pact idea, as we have seen, had been in the air since 1922, when Chancellor Cuno first suggested it; two more offers of such a pact were made by Stresemann in 1923, both of which were summarily rejected by Poincaré. But in 1924 the idea was taken up again, and this time seriously, not only because of the international events that had transpired since the last time the offer was made, but also because of changes within the political systems of Britain and France. In January 1924 Ramsay MacDonald came to power in Britain, and in June Herriot came to power in France. In both cases the shift was considered to be a mandate for change, although in Britain the change implied was less significant than in France. MacDonald and the Labor Party generally were committed to a policy of resolution of the security problem through League action in contrast to Curzon's rejection of the Draft Treaty; thus, they were enthusiastic supporters of the Geneva Protocol. Indeed, if MacDonald had remained in power, it is probable that this approach rather than that of Locarno would have been adopted. Herriot represented an abrupt about-face from Poincaré and stood for a return to cooperation with Britain and to diplomacy in place of military action. Yet the change represented by these elections should not be exaggerated; MacDonald still refused to adopt a strictly anti-German line, and Herriot had no intention of moving out of the Ruhr without adequate safeguards. A shift was discernible—but not a revolution—in foreign policy. It is doubtful that either MacDonald or Herriot would have ordered the quick evacuation of the Cologne zone at that time.

Yet there was movement. On June 17, 1924 Herriot, in a speech before the Chamber of Deputies, said that the security question could be resolved by a pact of guarantee under the League of Nations. Then, at a meeting between Herriot and MacDonald on June 21, 1924, MacDonald suggested that the military occupation of the Rhine be as limited as possible and the security question solved through the entry of Germany into the League. At the August meeting of the London Conference (on the Dawes Plan) Herriot brought up the subject of a security pact between France and Germany with Stresemann, who said there was no doubt it would be welcomed by Germany. At the same conference MacDonald and Stresemann discussed the problem of evacuating the Rhineland in general and especially the Cologne (first) zone. Finally, in September 1924, MacDonald made his famous empty-chair speech at the League of Nations, suggesting that Germany soon fill the chair held for it at the League.

The cogs were beginning to fall into place. Both Mac-

Donald and Herriot were seeking some way of formulating in concrete terms the more general demands of the internal political systems of their states. To fulfill those crudely formulated demands, the three brokers not only had to concern themselves with what their internal political system demanded but they also had to test, so to speak, the international system to see what it could yield. Thus, while the political and international situation of 1924 was dominated by the Dawes Plan on the one hand and the Geneva Protocol on the other, the three brokers continued to explore alternative means to resolving the problem of security.

As yet these were tentative and exploratory investigations. The main hope of Britain and France was still fixed on the Geneva Protocol because it fitted the demands of the Labor Party most perfectly, providing, as it did, a collective approach to the problem of security while at the same time giving a modicum of relief to French concerns about being left alone face-to-face with Germany. In order for the Locarno agreements to come into being, another shift of the internal political situation of Britain was required. This came about when the Labor Government fell in November 1924 and the Conservatives came back to power with Austen Chamberlain as foreign secretary. Without this change it is probable that the Labor Government would have ratified the Geneva Protocol and oriented British policy toward this more general and loosely organized form of security. But with Chamberlain's rejection of the Protocol, the whole question of European security in general and French security in particular was once again before the three powers. And if the soundings taken by the three brokers in the last half of 1924 had indicated that the demands of the three internal political systems might be fitted together, this task was still a difficult one, for those demands were still in sharp conflict with each other. It would take all the considerable skill of maneuver possessed by the three brokers to make a "deal." To understand the difficulties and the way they were overcome by a process of brokerage, it will be necessary to look at the issues from the point of view of each of the three brokers.

Stresemann

The most immediate issue facing Stresemann was the evacuation of the first zone of occupation. The refusal of the Allies to evacuate the Cologne zone on time was a threat both to his policy of restoring German territorial unity through freeing the Rhineland and to his policy of restoring German political unity through the satisfaction of German nationalism. With the lesson of the 1923 *Putsch* by Hitler before him, not to mention other efforts by the German nationalists to upset or weaken the Weimar Republic—including political murder—Stresemann understood only too well that nonevacuation of the Cologne zone would create a serious problem within Germany. As he put it, the "extremists will again get the upper hand." [18] To undercut their discontent, he also hoped to achieve some alleviation of the conditions within the two remaining zones of occupation in order to lift the heavy hand of the French military from the German population and to attain some reduction of the period of occupation of the two zones.

Yet Stresemann could not simply present a demand to the Allies that they evacuate the first Rhine zone and give concessions; a more subtle process of brokerage was necessary. He saw that while the evacuation of Cologne could come about through a security pact between the three states and that it would have to be explained to the Allied negotiators that the German Government would not agree to a pact without evacuation, it was at the same time necessary for the Germans to understand that that demand could not

[18] Eric Sutton, ed. and trans., *Gustav Stresemann: His Diaries, Letters, and Papers* (London, 1935–1940), Vol. I, p. 489. Hereafter cited as, Stresemann, *Papers*.

be made at the start of negotiations.[19] Stresemann, therefore, spent much of his energy preventing the German cabinet and the German political system in general from making demands that would not be met by the French or the
British or that would prevent their being realized if presented in a different way. To begin negotiations with the
demand that France withdraw from the Cologne zone was,
to Stresemann, simply a bad joke since such demands were
precisely what would make it least likely that the French
withdraw. He stated his problem clearly:

From the start the German government has presumed that
the French government will not be persuaded to withdraw
its forces unless France's so-called need for security is satisfied in some manner. The approach of the deadline of
January 10 has confronted France with the problem of
deciding whether to accommodate itself to the Allied Rhineland policy enunciated by the British and Americans at
Versailles over the opposition of French military interests,
or to preserve the possibility of pursuing further, even if
unilaterally, the plans of the military group. The present
government of France seems rather inclined toward the
first alternative. It is, however, unwilling—or, at any rate,
unable—to make and execute this decision without first
assuring France some substitute for the formal Anglo-
American guarantees which had been planned at Versailles
in 1919 but which had subsequently failed to materialize.
. . . France, of course, would be happiest if . . . a
Franco-Anglo-Belgian treaty could be concluded, strengthened by explicit military obligations on England's part.[20]

This shrewd understanding of French needs was what
Stresemann had to drive home to his not particularly intelligent political system. Since the German politician is
frequently not a man of subtle understanding, the idea that

[19] Stresemann, *Papers*, Vol. II, pp. 113, 134–136.
[20] Quoted by E. Eyck, *A History of the Weimar Republic* (Cambridge, Mass., 1963), Vol. II, p. 4.

the best way of getting the French to evacuate the Cologne zone was not to demand it would be a difficult one for him to grasp. And, in fact, the German nationalists never did grasp it. On the very eve of the Locarno Conference the nationalist press was insisting that Germany not attend the conference if the Cologne zone had not been evacuated beforehand, and it eventually forced Stresemann on September 26 to state Germany's claim for the immediate evacuation of the Cologne zone in the same note in which he accepted the invitation to the conference.[21] It is obvious that if the other two brokers had not had some understanding of the pressures to which Stresemann was subject, the conference would never have gotten under way—which is precisely what the nationalists wanted. Even so, Chamberlain was irritated; he and Briand simply refused to acknowledge this request; Stresemann himself privately asked Briand to ignore the demand expressed in the note.[22]

Stresemann was fully aware not only that he had to meet the French need for security but that he also had to help Britain meet the French need in a way that would be most favorable to Germany. It was clear that the failure of the Geneva Protocol would revive French requests for what would virtually be an Anglo-French alliance directed against Germany. He saw that the security problem would either be resolved by the Allies amongst themselves or in collaboration with Germany and that "a solution of this question without Germany would be a solution against Germany." [23] As Stresemann put it as early as February 19, 1924: "The problem of finding a formula . . . which will make it easier for the present French government to retreat from its position would be one well worth solving." [24] By making possible such a retreat, Stresemann could then set in motion

[21] Eyck, *Ibid.*, pp. 21–23.
[22] *Ibid.*, p. 23.
[23] Stresemann, *Papers*, Vol. II, p. 82.
[24] Stresemann, *Papers*, Vol. I, p. 286.

the plan that he hoped would achieve his main goal; that is, to create a condition of security that would protect Germany from French policy in general and the resumption of the Ruhr policy in particular by converting Britain from an ally of France to the holder of a balance between France and Germany. While Stresemann had no illusions about British affection toward Germany, he understood that, as a matter of self-interest, Britain wanted to avoid a solution to the security problem that would involve a tight alliance with France and, especially, involve a British commitment in Eastern Europe. Yet, Stresemann also feared Chamberlain's friendly attitude toward France, which, combined with British and French agreement not to evacuate the Cologne zone, held out the prospect that the policy of reconciliation between Germany and the Allies started by the Dawes Plan was coming to an end and that Germany would have little choice between isolation and alliance with Russia.[25] However, if Britain could be offered an alternative to the Anglo-French alliance, Stresemann would break through this threat of isolation and block the French scheme to acquire British backing and support for her alliances in Eastern Europe. As a result, Germany would establish a balance of power system in which Britain, as the holder of the balance, would prevent France from further extending her power in the East as well as in the West. But Germany could only achieve these objectives if she were sensitive to the needs and desires of France and Britain.

Some Germans were sensitive to these needs and desires, but most were not. Stresemann's role as a broker was to convince those who were opposed to meeting some of the French and British demands that they must do so in the interests of Germany. It was not an easy task, for what Stresemann had to do was make the DNVP and the public that supported it understand what could and what

[25] G. A. Craig, *From Bismarck to Adenauer: Aspects of German Statecraft* (Baltimore, 1958), pp. 74–76.

could not be done. The extremists—the Nazis, the Pan-German Union, the racists, all of whom said they would never abandon Alsace-Lorraine—were impossible to deal with. But the DNVP might be amenable to understanding. Stresemann tried to teach it the facts of international relations by a combination of persuasion and political manipulation. He tried to convince it, and other political parties and public opinion as well, of the logic of his approach through a series of meetings and public pronouncements in which he explained that the evacuation of Cologne and a shortening of the occupation in the rest of the Rhine could only be achieved by yielding to French demands in the West. More important, he executed a political turn to the right by bringing the DNVP into the cabinet and thus making the party responsible for the Locarno policy. It is worth pointing out that Stresemann was careful to explain his proposals to the various parties in terms of their own particular interests; with the Social Democrats (SPD) he pointed out that support of his proposals would help the left-wing government of Herriot; with the DNVP he pointed out that the pact would bring Britain to Germany's side in case of another Ruhr occupation and open up possibilities to the East.[26] So important was the inclusion of the DNVP in the cabinet in Stresemann's mind that he believed that without it the proposals for the security pact would not have been possible.[27] He also tried to work on right-wing German public opinion through the press, an effort that gradually swung the moderate parts of the DNVP more and more behind him.[28] At the same time that Stresemann found it necessary to include the DNVP in the German cabinet in order to make the party responsible, he also found their inclusion useful as a warning to France and Britain that if

[26] H. A. Turner, Jr., *Stresemann and the Politics of the Weimar Republic* (Princeton, 1963), p. 189.
[27] Stresemann, *Papers,* Vol. II, p. 76.
[28] Turner, *op. cit.,* pp. 210–211.

concessions were not forthcoming he would be pushed into the hands of the extreme nationalists.[29]

Stresemann had not only the German nationalists to contend with, but also General von Seeckt and the "Easterners." While Locarno was of great military advantage to Germany because it lowered Franco-German tensions and made the *Reichswehr*'s secret activities easier,[30] General von Seeckt, Chief of the German Army, was nevertheless against the pact because he was opposed to the whole idea of reconciliation with France. In a cabinet meeting von Seeckt had made his view clear when he said that "we must acquire power, and . . . as soon as we have power, we will naturally retake all that we have lost." [31] Hence he opposed the whole "Western" orientation of Stresemann's policy, fearing that it would lead to a destruction of the ties established between the German Army and Russia and weaken German power vis-à-vis the French and the Poles. There were others, too, who preferred an "Eastern" or Rapallo policy, including, it should be said, the German ambassador to Russia and the Russians themselves, who were so agitated about the prospects of the security pact that Soviet Commissar for Foreign Affairs Chicherin made trips to Berlin, Paris, and Warsaw in an effort to either threaten Germany with Polish-French-Russian friendship or cajole her with the prospects of joint action against the Poles.[32] Naturally, Stresemann did not hesitate to make use of the advantage that the Russians in their panic had given him; he was able to threaten the West with a close German-

[29] H. L. Bretton, *Stresemann and the Revision of Versailles* (Stanford, Calif., 1953), pp. 88–89.
[30] H. W. Gatzke, *Stresemann and the Rearmament of Germany* (Baltimore, 1954), p. 38.
[31] Quoted by Eyck, *op. cit.*, p. 10. See also G. A. Craig, *The Politics of the Prussian Army, 1640–1945* (New York, paperback ed., 1964), p. 422.
[32] For the complicated maneuvers of the Russians in this period see Korbel, *Poland between East and West;* Eyck, *op. cit.*, pp. 23–30.

Russian connection if there were no concessions forth-coming—a threat that was made plausible by the strong current of "Eastern" opinion within the Weimar Republic. It was quite a game, and Stresemann was playing it with marvelous skill.

He needed all the skill he possessed. While he had some success in bringing the leadership of the DNVP to under-stand what could and what could not be done, what Ger-many had to yield to France and Britain and what she could not demand, he nevertheless had great difficulty in making the internal political system of the Weimar Republic fit its demands to the facts of international life and even in keeping control over it. As one authority has put it, in the Weimar Republic, "to do what reason of state required without alienating public opinion was virtually impossible, as the careers of Rathenau, Stresemann, and Bruening demonstrate." [33] Stresemann was plagued throughout the month preceding the Locarno conference with attempts of the DNVP to escape responsibility for the security pact proposal—it claimed the proposal had originated with the foreign minister and not the cabinet—and by attempts to force his resignation. At one time Stresemann had to face Chancellor Luther with the choice of himself or the DNVP; it then appeared that Stresemann was virtually indispen-sable. The DNVP also constantly tried to make Stresemann demand extreme concessions from France, such as the prompt evacuation of the whole Rhine area, Allied accept-ance of Germany's intent to change boundaries in the East, and acceptance of the German repudiation of war guilt! [34] And, in fact, Stresemann did have to make a public state-ment before the Locarno Conference that Germany repudi-ated the war guilt clause—he also warned the British pri-

[33] Craig, *From Bismarck to Adenauer: Aspects of German Statecraft, op. cit.,* p. 61. Professor Craig points out that the defeat of Germany had resulted in greater control of the government by public opinion and legislature than before World War I, p. 60.
[34] Turner, *op. cit.,* p. 190.

vately that he would be doing so—since he was unable to prevent the DNVP from forcing him to make this crazy maneuver. His task was made even more complex by the election of Hindenburg as President of the Republic on April 26, 1925. Hindenburg was hardly a symbol of reconciliation or a man much calculated to make the French feel confidence in the pacific intentions of the German people. Stresemann was only too aware of the repercussions of this event abroad and opposed Hindenburg to the extent that he could, but the French, after an initial period of doubt, refused to let the election bring the negotiations to an end. Once again, Stresemann had to play the role of a broker, explaining to foreign opinion that Hindenburg was not the threat he might seem.[35]

Stresemann's attempts to bring the internal political system of the Weimar Republic to an understanding of his policy and what he thought was necessary for Germany was greatly harmed by the withdrawal of the DNVP from the German cabinet (October 23, 1925) because it would not accept the renunciation of Alsace-Lorraine implied by Locarno. As a result, the Locarno Treaties were ratified only with the aid of the SPD, which was not in the cabinet. Yet not all the DNVP was opposed to the pact; the opposition came mainly from the provincial organizations of the party. Many of the party leaders, and especially those businessmen and agriculturalists who saw economic advantages from trade with the West, and even von Seeckt, who finally realized that Germany's hands would not be tied in the East, eventually gave it support.[36] It was because of this support and the DNVP presence in the cabinet throughout most of the time that Stresemann was able to negotiate with comparative freedom.[37] Furthermore, if the DNVP refused to acknowledge the validity of the Locarno Treaties, Stresemann riposted by opposing the DNVP's reentrance into

[35] *Ibid.,* p. 199.
[36] *Ibid.,* p. 215.
[37] *Ibid.,* p. 218.

the cabinet until it made such an acknowledgment, which it did in early 1927. Certainly, it is clear that Stresemann played the broker's role effectively in the sense that he got the Locarno Treaties signed and ratified; whatever the ultimate success of his plans, that much was achieved. In addition he was able to shift opinion on the Right to some degree, even if not through a process of sweet reason. For the DNVP, or any other party except those on the Far Right, would have found it difficult to repudiate Locarno in practice once it was ratified. It even took Hitler three years to nerve himself and his generals to a repudiation of Locarno. But whatever estimate one may make of Stresemann's success—and we shall be concerned with that question in the last section of this chapter—it is clear that to arrive at the town of Locarno at all required the most skillful efforts of a skilled broker.

Stresemann's activity as a broker was not only to present the demands of France and Britain to the German political system but to present the demands of that system to France and Britain. As we have seen, the crucial German demand concerning the West involved the Rhine area. But there was also a crucial demand to be made by Germany concerning the East. However, even in this respect Stresemann had to play the role of modifier and to sensitize the German political system to the real possibilities in Eastern Europe. It was from this need to play the role of the broker in connection with Eastern Europe that much of the ambiguity of his Eastern policy came. The question of the nature of Stresemann's Eastern policy has been a subject of controversy, and deservedly so, because as a broker he had to deal with the problem on many levels. To the Allies he described his policy in one way; to the Germans in another way; and to the Russians in still another. One suspects that the essence of his policy at this time in the East was precisely ambiguity itself because any clear policy would have brought the whole Locarno negotiation to an end.

Yet on certain points Stresemann's presentation of German demands concerning Eastern Europe was anything but ambiguous because of the pressures of the German political system. No German foreign minister could have accepted a treaty system that in any way acknowledged the frontiers of Europe. Stresemann put it squarely to the French: Germany could not guarantee the borders of the Eastern states nor could she be a member of a series of Eastern arbitration treaties in which France was the guarantor. If France would not accept this position, there would be no Locarno. Further, Germany would not allow her obligations under the League of Nations, once she had joined, to put her in a position where she would be involved in a conflict with Russia under League auspices or where she must give transit rights to French troops to come to the aid of Poland. The idea of German aid to Poland in case of a Russian attack was obviously too painful for any German politician to contemplate. Hence, France must clearly accept German reservations concerning Article 16 of the League Covenant. At the same time Germany must be assured a permanent seat on the council of the League; this would enable her to protect the German minority in Poland through League action, especially since Poland was not a permanent member of the council. This final demand was accepted by France and Britain, but it triggered off an awesome wrangle in the League itself over who should sit and for how long.

The ambiguity at the heart of the German position lay in the doubt as to what Germany—and Stresemann—were planning to do in the East in general and about the Polish frontier in particular. Manifestly, Stresemann fought and fought successfully against a strengthening of French influence in this area, but what did this mean for German power in that area? So important is this question to the balance of power in Europe that it will have to be considered later in connection with the Locarno balance as a whole. Here it can simply be said that Stresemann played his role as a broker not only in getting France and Britain to accept the demand of the German political system that Germany not have its hands tied in the East, but he also played that role by refusing to allow the "Easterners" to dominate policy and to orient Germany toward the East.

Briand

Compared with Stresemann, the positions of Briand and Chamberlain were relatively simple. The failure of the Ruhr occupation had left France with the need to restore her relations with Britain and to prevent Britain from breaking front with France. At the same time the state of French politics would not allow Herriot and later Briand[38] to concede the French position on the Rhine without some significant concession from Germany. The 1924 election had made it possible for France to make concessions; it had not made it possible for France simply to change her whole stance toward Germany. Indeed, the first reaction of France to Britain's disavowal of the Geneva Protocol was not to come to terms with Germany but to attempt a revival of the Anglo-French treaty in order to bring about an alliance with the British against Germany; Herriot had no illusions about Germany, for he told Chamberlain (March 7, 1925): "I tell you I look forward with terror to her [Germany] making war upon us again in ten years." [39]

The prime task that faced Herriot and Briand was not only to present the demands of the French internal system to the British but also the demands of Britain to the French. Oddly enough, the existence of a Conservative government in Britain and a "Left" government in France helped to

[38] Herriot was both Prime Minister and foreign minister from June 14, 1924 to April 16, 1925. Briand was either Prime Minister and foreign minister together or foreign minister from April 16, 1925 to January 13, 1932.
[39] Sir C. Petrie, *The Life and Letters of the Right Honorable Sir Austen Chamberlain* (London, 1939–1940), Vol. II, p. 263.

LOCARNO AND THE MAKING OF A BALANCE 89

further the process of brokerage. The reason for this state of affairs was simply that the French Left was more willing to conciliate Germany and adopt a policy of conciliation in general in Europe as well as to support the League than was the Right. The tradition of the French Right in international affairs was to act independently in Europe and to use force to coerce the rest of Europe rather than conciliate other states, including both Britain and Germany.[40] Thus, while the coming to power of Herriot and Briand did not permit the French Government to turn its destinies over to Britain, it did make it easier for it to act as a go-between for the British and French political systems and to redefine or modify the French demands in the light of British demands.

French policy during the Locarno negotiations centered around the two key problems of German demands for changes in the Rhine and the role of the states of Eastern Europe in the French security system. On the Rhine issue French policy was to link evacuation of the Cologne zone with security and to make sure that security was achieved first. Thus, France refused to promise to evacuate the Cologne zone before and even during the Locarno Conference, the promise came only after the conference was concluded. Yet Briand found it necessary to take cognizance of German demands and to meet them to a degree. The French scrupulously met the promise given to Stresemann as a result of the Dawes negotiations that the Ruhr would be evacuated by August 1, 1925; coming as it did during the negotiations over the terms of Locarno, the evacuation strengthened the hand of Stresemann as against his nationalist opponents.[41] Also, Briand and Chamberlain timed the announcement of their evacuation of the Cologne zone so that it would become public just previous to the ratification debate in Germany. Thus Briand had to combine an appreciation of the demands made by the internal systems *both* of France and

[40] J. P. T. Bury, *France, 1814–1940* (London, 1959), p. 264.
[41] Eyck, *op. cit.*, p. 20.

Germany as well as of Britain and balance off their demands one against the other. Needless to say, the brokers of the other two states made sure he understood this necessity.[42]

It was in connection with the problem of Eastern Europe that Herriot and Briand found it most difficult to play the role of broker. As one authority has put it, "whether Stresemann liked it or not, the battle in France was now centered on the issue which his proposal had deliberately excluded, namely security in East Central Europe." [43] For here the French brokers had to balance not only the demands of the French, British, and German political systems, but also of their allies in East Europe, Poland and Czechoslovakia. At the beginning of the negotiations, France seized the opportunity offered by the pact proposals to use them as a means of freezing the borders of Eastern Europe and strengthening the status quo in that area through new legal obligations on the part of Germany. France attempted to do this by insisting that the new pact not impair the League of Nations or the Versailles Treaty in any way and that the arbitration treaties between Germany, Poland, and Czechoslovakia be guaranteed by France in the same manner that Britain was the guarantor in the West.[44] The object was to connect the arrangements made in both areas so that France could intervene in the East and to lay down the rule that the acceptance of the status quo by France in the West did not mean that she could not come to the aid of her Eastern allies by virtue of an attack on Germany in the West.[45] Needless to say, such a proposition was unacceptable to Stresemann.[46] Such a system of guarantees would mean, in Stresemann's view, that France would be in a position to decide unilaterally when she should act and when aggression

[42] See Stresemann, *Papers,* Vol. II, pp. 91–93.
[43] Wandcyz, *op. cit.,* p. 331.
[44] See British Parliamentary Paper Cmd. 2435 (1925) for the French reply to Stresemann's original note proposing the security pact.
[45] Wandcyz, *op. cit.,* p. 348.
[46] Stresemann, *Papers,* Vol. II, p. 95; Wandcyz, *op. cit.,* p. 352.

in the East had taken place, an obvious invitation to France to secure a legal right to attack Germany in the West. In short, Stresemann saw Briand as trying to work the Franco-Polish pact into the Western pact.

Stresemann was rescued from the threat of this demand by the British, as he had foreseen. France had tried to involve the British in their guarantee of the East, but Chamberlain rejected the idea that Britain participate in the arbitration treaties.[47] Thus, the French gradually had to yield, and by September had come around to the view that if the Germans refused to make France the guarantor of the treaties of arbitration between Germany, Poland, and Czechoslovakia, France would guarantee Poland and Czechoslovakia on her own.[48] This shift required some expert brokerage activities from Briand if Poland and Czechoslovakia were to be satisfied. Poland, in particular, was deeply concerned; yet the Polish foreign minister had to recognize that too much pressure on France would force the French to choose between East and West; he too, therefore, had to play a broker's role and "prepare the Polish public for acceptance of arrangements that might be unavoidable, while simultaneously . . . trying to safeguard Poland's interest by pressure on Paris. . . ."[49] Czechoslovakia, on the other hand, took a more positive attitude toward the pact, since Beneš saw it as providing a general *detente* in Europe and not as posing a specific threat to his state because the Germans had told him that they did not contemplate any changes in the German-Czech frontier.[50] Briand's task was, therefore, relatively easy in respect to Czechoslovakia; in respect to Poland, however, while he tried to demonstrate French solidarity he nevertheless left the Polish government with a sense of uneasiness.[51]

[47] See British Parliamentary Paper Cmd. 2435 (1925), pp. 18–19.
[48] Wandcyz, *op. cit.*, p. 355.
[49] *Ibid.*, p. 334.
[50] *Ibid.*, pp. 350–351, 336–337.
[51] *Ibid.*, pp. 354–355.

These negotiations took place against a background of controversy within France on the proposed pact; the Socialists were enthusiastic about the pact, but the Right, including Poincaré, was vehemently opposed. At the same time, the government was deeply involved in a financial crisis and in troubles in Syria. It was precisely because of these divisions that the French were in such a weak position vis-à-vis Britain and Germany; Poincaré might rant and rave, but the fact of the matter was that the French Chamber had refused to vote him the money necessary for continuing the Ruhr occupation, and the French electorate had voted his group out of office. Yet Briand also was in a weak position. While he would have been pleased to commit the British to a firm line over Eastern Europe, his main role in these negotiations was not to coerce the British or Germans—he had little with which to coerce them —but to exact as much of the French demand as was possible from them and at the same time to bring the French political system to face the reality of the path they had chosen. To do so, he had to play the only strong suit he had with the French public, namely the fact that he had gained a British guarantee of the Rhine.

Chamberlain

Once the German Government had proposed the security pact, it was Chamberlain's task to use the opportunity it offered to act as a broker between the other two statesmen and also between their demands and the demands of the British political system. As we have seen, the British were loath—to put it mildly—to join an Anglo-French pact. Yet with the rejection of the Geneva Protocol,[52] there seemed to be little alternative; indeed, even if the Geneva

[52] See British Parliamentary Paper Cmd. 2368 (1925) for Chamberlain's statement to the League of Nations on the Geneva Protocol and his reasons for rejecting it.

Protocol had been accepted by the British, the French would have continued to make further demands on them.[53] Even after the official proposal of the Rhineland Treaty by Stresemann in February 1925, the French continued to press the British for a pact between the two states; without such a pact, they claimed, French public opinion would not be satisfied, since they would see the Rhineland Treaty only as a reaffirmation of Versailles rather than as a solution to the security problem. But Germany would not join the Rhineland Treaty if it was accompanied by another pact from which she was excluded. Hence, on March 7 Chamberlain informed the French Prime Minister that an Allied pact was unacceptable to British public opinion and advised him to work on the German proposal.[54] In so doing, Chamberlain was at one and the same time acting to present what he at least considered to be the demands of his own political system for a limited engagement in Europe and to act as a go-between, or, as he put it, as an honest broker, between France and Germany.

Chamberlain's own reaction to Stresemann's proposal was that of tempered enthusiasm:

I am firmly convinced that the true line of progress is to proceed from the particular to the general, and not, as has hitherto been embodied in Covenant and Protocol, to reverse the process and eliminate the particular by the general. A form of guarantee which is so general that we undertake exactly the same obligations in defense, shall I say of the Polish Corridor (for which no British Government ever will or ever can risk the bones of a British grenadier) as we extend to those international arrangements or conditions, upon which, as our history shows, our national existence depends, is a guarantee so wide and general that it carries no conviction whatever and gives no sense of security to those who are concerned in our action.[55]

[53] Petrie, op. cit., p. 256.
[54] Ibid., p. 263.
[55] Chamberlain to Lord Crewe, February 16, 1925, ibid., pp. 258–260.

Yet, at the same time, he saw obstacles in Britain in the way of a "particular" arrangement; public opinion in general and the Labor Party, the Liberal Party, and the League of Nations Union especially were all against such arrangements. To add to his problems, the armed services and the Foreign Office were in favor of an alliance with France.[56] The situation was made even more complicated by the desire of the "ordinary citizen" and the rank and file of the Conservative Party to avoid a commitment to Europe.[57] But by April, not only the cabinet but what Chamberlain called a "growing body of public opinion" supported his policy; even Ramsay MacDonald was willing to consider alternatives other than the Geneva Protocol.[58]

One of the most important factors working in favor of Chamberlain was the freedom of action he possessed due to lack of interest in, and lack of knowledge of, foreign affairs on the part of Stanley Baldwin, Prime Minister at that time. Evidently, Baldwin hoped that the Locarno Treaty would end the whole problem of British involvement in Europe, and that once the treaties had been concluded, the problem would be settled for good.[59] With this backing, Chamberlain was in a strong position to impose his solution on the British political system thanks to party discipline. But even so, he was aware that he could go so far and no further.

The so far and no further was especially imperative with regard to the question of the Eastern frontiers and the *casus foederis* of the Rhine security pact. In respect to the Eastern question, Chamberlain found it necessary to impose upon —or, if one prefers, impress upon—the French the limits beyond which the British would not go. Thus, at the same time that he offered the French security on the Rhine, he

---

[56] *Ibid.*, pp. 254–255, 258–260.
[57] *Ibid.*, p. 260.
[58] *Ibid.*, pp. 271–274.
[59] See G. A. Craig and Felix Gilbert, eds., *The Diplomats* (New York, 1963), Vol. I, pp. 40–42; see also Stresemann, *Papers*, Vol. III, pp. 229, 262, for evidence of post-Locarno British isolationism.

had to modify French expectations in the East. In doing so, he also acted in the interests of the German Government, but also, he felt, in the interests of the French Government. In Chamberlain's view security in the West would bring about security in the East: "In obtaining additional security in the West, I think we do in fact lessen the danger of war in the East. . . ." [60]

The basis of this judgment was that Germany would enter the League of Nations and renounce anything but peaceful action in her search for a redress of grievances. On a more general level, Chamberlain hoped and assumed that an improvement of Franco-German relations, which would be brought about by the Western pact, would lead to a greater sense of French security and hence lessen France's fears about what would happen in the East. For Chamberlain was not indisposed to some sort of change in the East, or, as he put it, "a friendly arrangement" made directly between the Poles and the Germans. And what did that mean? It is hard to know because Chamberlain also wanted to make it clear that Britain was not in favor of destroying any of the existing treaty stipulations "in regard to the Eastern frontiers." [61] Yet he also said that he did not expect Germany to "renounce formally all hope that time and diplomacy may lead to some modification of the arrangements in the East." He went on to add that "for the moment I think the less that is said about the East the better it will be." [62] In the light of his own ambivalence, one can see his point.

Chamberlain was certainly acting the role of broker to the hilt. Was he also acting honestly? Despite the appearance of confusion and/or double-dealing, he was undoubtedly honest in his aims. For as a broker, what he was trying to do was to achieve security for France within the

[60] Petric, *op. cit.*, pp. 267–268.
[61] See the letters of Chamberlain, March 18, 1925 and April 2, 1925, in Petrie, *op. cit.*, pp. 267–268, 271–274.
[62] Letter of April 2, 1925, *ibid.*, pp. 271–274. See also letter of March 18, 1925.

narrow limits established by the British political system and
to bring France and Germany together in order that eventually the Eastern question would no longer be seen as a
threat to France. Once that state of affairs had been
achieved, the question would, hopefully, solve itself and
Germany and Poland could come to an amicable agreement because the problem could be discussed in a framework in which tension between France and Germany was
absent. Until that time—a "reasonable number of years,"
in Chamberlain's phrase—what he hoped for was a moratorium on the Eastern question, a moratorium he thought
he had attained in Germany's promise to take only peaceful steps to achieve her foreign policy objectives in the
East as well as in the West.

Throughout this complicated game—as Chamberlain
said, "a three-handed game, such as is now going on between Paris, Berlin, and London, is not an easy one to
play" [63]—Chamberlain was quite specific on the point
that Britain would not guarantee the Eastern frontiers herself. He told the Poles in March[64] that he would not do so,
and he informed the French in May that the Eastern arbitration treaties and the Rhine pact were distinct categories
as far as Britain was concerned.[65] He also made it clear
that the *casus foederis* for the Rhine pact should not involve Britain in an instantaneous reaction but that a process
of arbitration should take place before a resort to force
occurred. Only in the case of a "flagrant act," constituting
an "immediate danger" to the other states, would a resort
to force be justified without exhausting the processes of
conciliation. Chamberlain gave as an example of a flagrant
act the marching of German armies into or troops being
assembled in the demilitarized zone.[66] Thus, the limits of

---

[63] *Ibid.*, pp. 258–260.
[64] *Ibid.*, p. 266.
[65] *Ibid.*, pp. 276–277.
[66] See Chamberlain's statement in his letter of August 11, 1925 to
D'Abern, *ibid.*, pp. 281–283. See also Chamberlain's statement in
 of Commons, June 24, 1925.

British involvement were made clear to the French. At the same time, British intent was spelled out so that they and the Germans would not be deceived and could plan accordingly. It was further made clear that the guarantee applied to both Germany and France; that is, in case of a French attack on Germany, the British would apply the same standards as in the case of a German attack on France.

Chamberlain's role as broker was, as he himself saw, vital to the making of Locarno. The main thrust of this role was to convince the British public that a commitment to France was necessary, that isolationism must be given up, and to convince France that Germany must be treated as an equal, that French security lay not only with Britain and the states of Eastern Europe but also in stable Franco-German relations.

The Locarno Conference

Although solutions to the crucial issues had been outlined before the meeting at Locarno, the final acts of brokerage occurred at the conference itself (October 15–16, 1925), at which three fundamental conflicts were finally resolved: those over the arbitration treaties in the East, the question of Article 16 of the League Covenant, and the problem of the evacuation of the Cologne zone. On the arbitration treaties the issue was the one that the British, the French, and the Germans had already discussed, namely, whether or not France should act as a guarantor of the arbitration treaties signed between Germany, Poland, and Czechoslovakia just as Britain acted as the guarantor for the West. On this issue Briand was forced to give way; without British support, there was little else he could do. Besides, Briand was convinced by this time of the need for the security pact[67] and had gone so far along the road to Locarno that it would be difficult to back out. The resulting treaties contained no recognition by Germany of the borders of Poland and Czechoslovakia and were not guaranteed by other states.[68] As far as Article 16 was concerned, it was agreed that Germany possess an escape clause as a member of the League of Nations.[69]

These two decisions had essentially been arrived at before the conference. There was one major problem, however, which remained unsolved. The Rhine issue was clearly of crucial importance, not only to Stresemann, for without significant concessions his whole domestic policy would have been in ruins, but to the whole concept of Locarno. It was at the heart of the Locarno bargain, which was that Germany would give France security in the West and a promise of peaceful behavior in the East in return for evacuation of the first (Cologne) zone and the hope of rapid evacuation of the other two zones. In making his demand for changes in the Rhine, Stresemann was presenting the bill given to him by the internal political system of Germany.

The brokerage that brought these two positions together emerged from the originally strong demand that Stresemann had put forth at Locarno; he told Briand that there was no longer any reason for French troops in the Rhine since France now had achieved security. On hearing this, Briand, according to Stresemann, "almost fell off the sofa."[70] Chamberlain was no less astonished, but agreed that the matter of Cologne should be cleared up before the security

---

[67] See Wandcyz, op. cit., pp. 359–360. See also Stresemann, Papers, Vol. II, pp. 173–175, 198, 216–221; British Parliamentary Paper Cmd. 2525 (1925); Royal Institute of International Affairs, Survey of International Affairs (London, 1925 ff.), Vol. II, p. 52; Eyck, op. cit., pp. 34–35.

[68] Wandcyz, op. cit., pp. 362–363.

[69] Stresemann, Papers, Vol. II, p. 199; Eyck, op. cit., p. 34.

[70] Quoted by Gatzke, op. cit., p. 41.

pact could be realized.[71] Having made his extreme demand,
Stresemann became more realistic. He suggested not only
what he should say in the note that would be delivered to
the Allies on the problems and progress of German disarmament and that would justify Allied withdrawal from
the first zone, but what the Allies were to say in reply. Both
Chamberlain and Briand agreed to this procedure.[72] Accordingly, on November 8, Stresemann was informed in-
formally by the British ambassador that the evacuation of
Cologne would probably begin on December 1; in reply
Stresemann urged the need for concessions in the occupation procedures in the other two zones. On November 14
an Allied note set December 1 as the date for the beginning
of the evacuation of the Cologne zone, described the measures to be taken to alleviate the occupation in the remainder
of the Rhineland, and stated that there would be a reduction in the size of the Allied Control Commission, which
presumably was overseeing German disarmament.[73] It is
noteworthy that these concessions came before the Reichstag debate on the ratification of the Locarno Treaties on
November 23–27. It is also noteworthy that at the London
Conference of December 1, at which the Locarno Treaties
were signed, Stresemann did not dare speak to Britain and
France about shortening the occupation period of the second and third zones of the Rhine because "we should only
have invited a refusal." [74] However, he did not refrain from
returning to the question in later years.

These concessions on the Rhine were made with Allied
knowledge that Germany was evading the disarmament provisions of Versailles.[75] Yet the virtual end of military con-

[71] See Stresemann, *Papers,* Vol. II, pp. 179–181, 183, 185–188.
[72] Gatzke, *op. cit.,* p. 41.
[73] See British Parliamentary Paper Cmd. 2527 (1925) for the correspondence on this subject.
[74] Stresemann, *Papers,* Vol. II, p. 237.
[75] Eyck, *op. cit.,* pp. 46–47; Gatzke, *op. cit.,* Ch. I and p. 46 ff.

trol and the evacuation of the Cologne zone, despite the
fact that legally the Allies should have stayed there, was
part of the brokerage of Locarno. It was a direct concession on the part of Britain and especially France to the
demands of the German political system once Stresemann
had modified those demands.

The Creative Role of Brokerage

The emphasis in this discussion of Locarno has been on
the ways in which the foreign ministers of Britain, France,
and Germany reacted to each other's demands and to the
demands of the internal political systems of the three
states.[76] It could, therefore, easily seem that the foreign
ministers-as-brokers were essentially passive in the process
of policymaking, that they transmitted and modified demands but did not originate them. Such is manifestly not
true. The foreign ministers did not simply transmit and
modify; they were the truly creative element in the process
that led to Locarno. Indeed, their role as brokers *forced*
them to be the creative element for at least three reasons.
First, they knew more about the problems that had to be
resolved and the political environment necessary for their
resolution than did anyone else. (Of course, lack of knowledge never kept any interested person from giving his views
on foreign affairs, but it does tend to become a handicap
when it comes to dealing with the concrete facts of policy.)
As a result, the brokers were in command of the situation
and possessed wide powers of discretion based on the fact

[76] The concentration on these three men has been mainly for the
sake of convenience and because they were the crucial decision-
makers. However, it is both unrealistic and unfair not to recognize
that each was surrounded by foreign policy advisers who were of
great importance in policy formation. This was especially true of
France and Germany, where the permanent officials such as Berthelot
and Maltzan were extremely significant in aiding their chiefs in the
making of policy. See Craig and Gilbert, *op. cit.*, Vol. I.

of superior knowledge alone. Indeed, it was precisely this superior knowledge, which no one else had to such a degree, that forced them to make choices and invent policies. It was because each of the three individuals under consideration knew so many of the facts about the position of his own country *and the position of the other states involved* that he not only felt the need to act but decided to act in a particular way. Others may have drawn different conclusions from the same set of facts, but few at that time possessed the same set of facts. Ignorance is seldom a source of creativity, but knowledge almost always is. It was knowledge that Stresemann, Briand, and Chamberlain had in abundance. On the basis of that knowledge they felt a need to deal with the problems presented by Europe in the years 1924–1925 and were able to invent a new solution—good, bad, or indifferent as it might have been—which dealt concretely and in detail with those problems. Anyone in their position would have been forced to do the same, although with probably different results. But it is exactly their position as brokers that is significant, for that was the crucial source of their creativity.

Second, the brokers alone were capable of translating the vague and contradictory demands of the internal political systems into concrete and realistic policies. As we have seen, the internal political system of any state, by the very nature of its diffuse characteristics, can only state its demands in general terms, which in and of themselves are not operational and are susceptible to a wide variety of interpretations. What goes on within the political parties and what issues forth from Parliament, the Chamber of Deputies, and the Reichstag may be a mandate, but the gulf between this mandate and what is actually done in international relations is large. The broker is the one who crosses it. His role in this respect is especially important when the demands made upon him are contradictory or confused. The French electorate wanted Germany to be kept or made weak *and* to reduce taxes; it ejected Poin-

caré because he raised taxes due to the needs of the Ruhr
occupation. Yet it in no way wished the French Government to ease up on Germany by, for example, an early
evacuation of German territory. (This was, of course, especially true of the French military leaders.) What, in these
circumstances, was Briand to do? He tried to achieve as
much as possible of both demands, but to do that meant
to work within a real situation where, as we have seen, he
had to invent a policy that would bring together those demands and the facts of international life. This was his
creative contribution to French foreign policy. The same
was true of Chamberlain and Stresemann. The broker is,
in a very real sense, an artist who combines given materials
into new forms. (It is hardly necessary to say, of course,
that some artists are competent and others are not.) The
materials themselves determine the results, but only in a
very general way.

Finally, and most important, because the broker is at-
tuned to what is going on inside his own and other states,
he has his own ideas of what should be done and infuses
these ideas into his policy along with the other elements
that go into its making. The broker is not only a politician
who knows how to respond to demands and how to bring
a policy out of them. He is also someone who has given
some thought to the problems with which he must deal
and who usually has a relatively clear-cut concept of how
they should be resolved—usually more clear-cut than the
ideas held by most other individuals within the political
system. He is not naive enough to think that he can achieve
this policy without taking into consideration the demands
of others. But he is not so neutral or passive that he does
not have certain concrete aims of his own. These aims become especially important when the internal political system of which he is a part does not make clear-cut demands
or when its demands are so vague as to be almost meaning-
less. In certain circumstances the internal political system
may even be unaware or uninterested in a particular ques-

tion of foreign policy, or, if interested and aware, may be baffled about what should be done. It is in such cases that the creative, or innovative, role of the broker assumes special importance, for the definition of national interest lies almost entirely in his hands. But even where the internal political system is relatively precise and unified in its demands, the broker will find it possible, and indeed necessary, to put into practice his own specific views on a foreign policy. Each of the three brokers studied here was motivated by certain concrete ideas about what should be done in the Europe of 1925. For various reasons, each of them wanted to find some way of resolving the Franco-German conflict through a process of conciliation and revisionism. In each case this approach was based on a particular attitude toward the national interest, but in each case also it was a special idea of what the national interest was or how it could be achieved in the particular situation of 1925 that dominated the thinking of these three men. Locarno was, in a very real sense, the personal achievement of Chamberlain, Driand, and Stresemann.

The Locarno Balance

The general nature and outline of the Locarno balance is not difficult to discern. What might be called the "Locarno Bargain," arranged by the three brokers, released the pressure of France on Germany in return for which France was promised security by Britain and Germany against a German attack. The balance that came out of this bargain was characterized by a limited rebirth of German power and a limited decline in French power; this equalization process was controlled and checked by Britain as the holder of the balance; British power could maintain the balance by its explicit threat to support either state should the other attempt to transgress those limits. Obviously, those limits were difficult to define with precision, and obviously too, it is difficult even today to know precisely how "equal" France and Germany had become as a result of Locarno. But it is clear that both on paper and in practice France had been constrained from adventuring on another Ruhr occupation, while Germany was forced to realize that a future attack on France was not within the realm of possibility as long as the Locarno balance held.

It is easy to assume that because Hitler did attack France in 1940 the Locarno Treaties were not only ineffective but an illusion, that they did not establish a balance but rather allowed the development of German hegemony. The question of the circumstances under which Hitler attacked France and the problem presented to Hitler by British support of France must be postponed for the following chapter. Here it need only be said that not until Hitler had established military control in the East did he feel he could attack France directly with his armies in 1940. The crucial problem that Locarno raises, therefore, is the question of German power in Eastern Europe and the effect of Locarno on the relationships between Germany and Eastern Europe. Did Locarno open the way to an expansion of Germany in the East of such a nature and extent that in fact it undermined the balance of power established by Locarno?

This question leads us to one of the most difficult aspects of international relations, that of estimating the intentions of a state. To answer that question it is necessary to understand the motives of Germany *at that time,* and especially the motives of Stresemann and those who might succeed him. It is also necessary to understand what was a reasonable forecast of the future *in 1925.* What would Germany do in Eastern Europe with its new power? What would Stresemann do? Who would be most likely to succeed Stresemann, and what would he try to do in the East? What did the future of European diplomacy look like in 1925 to the brokers who made Locarno, and were their estimates reasonable?

That Germany ached to restore the lost provinces that

had been given to Poland cannot be doubted and was not doubted at the time. The problem was, how would she go about it? As far as Stresemann is concerned, a controversy has grown up since the end of World War II over his honesty and his motives in making Locarno.[77] Because it has been discovered that he misled or tried to mislead—that is, lied to—Briand about the secret rearmament of Germany and that he condoned such rearmament,[78] it has been realized that whatever Stresemann was, he was no dove of peace. Certainly, it is clear that he was a German patriot first, and that he desired to see Germany restored to great power status. It is also clear that he desired to see Germany expand in Eastern Europe in general and, more specifically, eventually to find some way of revising the German-Polish border. Recognizing this, however, it is also necessary to ask how he would achieve these objectives and what limits if any he would put on them. Stresemann's policies after Locarno make it clear that he intended to expand German influence in Eastern Europe through economic pressures, that he intended to fight for the rights of Germans in Poland (and elsewhere) through the League of Nations, that he hoped to weaken Poland through economic attrition so that she would eventually be forced to make concessions to Germany, and that he hoped for an eventual *Anschluss* with Austria. It is also clear that he realized that Locarno made all this possible but that it also prevented the use of military force in any foreseeable future in Eastern Europe to achieve these objectives. Stresemann's aims, therefore, in Eastern Europe can be summarized as expanding Germany's political and economic influence in that area and a revision—the degree of which would be left to circumstances at the time—of the German-Polish border. Eastern Europe was to become a Ger-

---

[77] See H. W. Gatzke, "Gustav Stresemann: A Bibliographical Article," *Journal of Modern History* (March 1964), for a discussion of recent literature on Stresemann.

[78] See Gatzke, *Stresemann and the Rearmament of Germany*.

man sphere of influence, not an area of conquest. It was
not to become an area of conquest not because Stresemann
had moral qualms on the subject (although he would probably have had more than some Germans), but because
Locarno did not give him one of the crucial necessities for
such a conquest, namely, an expanded *Reichswehr* and
military occupation of the Rhineland. Indeed, Locarno,
through British insistence, brought a pledge from Germany
that only peaceful means would be used in the pursuit of
change in Eastern Europe. Further, the Rhine was to continue to be demilitarized, and the British specifically noted
that any mobilization of German troops in the Rhine would
be a flagrant violation of Locarno, to be acted upon immediately by the British without the prior sanction of the
League. As long as the Rhine was demilitarized, Germany
could not move Eastward with her troops for fear of a
French move into the Rhine-Ruhr area.

The British, as the holders of the balance, were a significant factor, therefore, in German calculations about Eastern Europe. They were a significant factor not only because
they blocked the way to certain methods but also because
they opened the way to other methods. Chamberlain saw
no reason why Germany should not expand her influence
in Eastern Europe. Nor did he see any reason why there
should not eventually be changes in the German-Polish border that were peacefully made with the consent of both
parties. Such an attitude is not as naive as might first appear. Chamberlain realized that German power could not
be prevented from expansion in Eastern Europe without a
price that the British public would not pay. More important, Chamberlain assumed that if Locarno held a balance
for a number of years and maintained stability in Europe,
then Germany and the states of Eastern Europe would
come to some kind of mutual understanding, passions
would cool, and reasonable changes could be made. Over
time, fear of Germany in Eastern Europe and the desires
of Germany in that area would each abate somewhat.

To say that this is a typical example of British optimism, pragmatism, naiveté, and lack of understanding of the passions of Eastern Europe is easy, but incorrect. To say that this is the view held by Chamberlain because he had no other choice due to British quasi-isolationism holds some truth, but is still basically incorrect. For the fact of the matter is that in 1925 there was every reason to assume that future European diplomacy might well achieve such ends. True, there was risk: one could not be certain that such would be the case. But that was all the more reason to establish Locarno so that the forecast would have a better chance of coming true. The hope was that German power would be restrained and limited, that other states would learn to come to terms with it and Germany to come to terms with other states. And there were good grounds to believe that German power would be restrained, grounds that went beyond the personality of Stresemann, though that was a not unimportant factor. One basis for this hope was the new economic prosperity that Europe discovered after 1925 and that it was reasonable to assume would continue. Another was the belief that the Weimar Republic, though racked by the fantasies of the German nationalists, would be consolidated and achieve a degree of stability. If it did, a German attack on Eastern Europe would hardly be likely, if for no other reason than the fact that the German Social Democrats would veto such an expansion of German military influence. In this connection it is worth pointing out that one reason for Stresemann himself being so limited in his concrete objectives in Eastern Europe was that he could not have acquired unified support for military expansion at home due to the power of the SPD in the Reichstag.

The reasonableness of these assumptions, and hence the stability of the Locarno balance itself, can be demonstrated by raising two "if" questions. What would have happened *if* prosperity had continued? The answer to this first question is that most probably the diplomatic situation would have turned out the way Chamberlain had hoped it would, since the Weimar Republic would have consolidated itself to a degree at least and German expansion in the East have followed the Chamberlain prescription. If it had not, French power was not so weak that it could not act in Eastern Europe—a fact demonstrated in 1931, even after the Depression had set in, when France forced Germany to withdraw from an Austro-German customs union. But let us assume the worst, short of the rise to power of Hitler. What would have happened *if* the German army had attempted to establish a military dictatorship under, say, Kurt von Schleicher, as the latter fondly hoped to do in 1932? The answer to this second question is that quite possibly there would have been a rise of tension in Eastern Europe and a German-Polish border war would have broken out. Such a war would have been a limited one, and while it might have led to a wider war, it is more probable that it would not have. Poland would have suffered from another partition and made painful sacrifices, as she has so often done for European peace. Anglo-French mediation would have seen to it that she made such sacrifices but also that something was saved from the wreck. Would German military expansion then have continued? To answer that question adequately we must consider the attitudes of the German military leaders, as we will do in the next chapter, but for now it can be said that it is doubtful. As we shall see, even Hitler could hardly nerve himself to plunge into the cataclysm of World War II. Certainly few German military leaders had much of a stomach for a second world war.

Locarno as a balance of power may not receive one's moral approbation. By substituting a limited German power and domination in Eastern Europe for limited French power and domination, with time it would undoubtedly have strengthened the position and influence of German industrial and military groups in Eastern Europe, and hence in Europe as a whole; given the nature of these groups, it is legitimate to have moral doubts about such a development. Yet if Locarno had succeeded, the Weimar Republic might well have been strengthened and the Social Democrats placed in a more secure and advantageous position within Germany. But whatever moral stance one may take about Locarno, it is nevertheless true that a viable and stable balance had been created, which held considerable promise of diplomatic and international stability in Europe.

But Locarno was viable and stable only as long as the conditions upon which it was based were valid. These conditions continued to be valid even past the crash of 1929 and until 1933 or perhaps even 1936. But when those conditions changed, Locarno—which was no more eternally valid than any other work of politics—ceased to function in its original form, and modifications to it or a new balance of power was required. It is not, therefore, legitimate and accurate to ask, why the Locarno balance failed. The question that must be asked is why the brokers of the 1930's failed to make the modifications required in the Locarno balance or to create a new balance when the assumptions on which Locarno was based had vanished.

As we have seen, the Locarno balance was to a very considerable degree the work of the brokers themselves as they combined the various conflicting attitudes and policies of the three states into a workable plan. A balance of power is not a law of nature; it does not occur automatically because of the operation of abstract "forces" or because of the manipulations of an invisible hand. Quite the contrary, it is the work of highly visible hands; those of Chamberlain, Briand, and Stresemann in the case of Locarno. An analysis of international relations in the 1930's will show the task faced by the broker as the active element in making a balance when there is a threat to the balance of power as a system of ordering international relations. What can brokerage accomplish if there is a threat to the balance from a major state that is a partner to an already existing balance? In such a situation, how can brokerage be used to preserve the balance and thus prevent the outbreak of war?

In answering this question, attention must be focused on the position of Britain, not only because she was the most powerful opponent of Hitler, but because of her role as the holder of the balance, which emerged from Locarno. In this role Britain could throw her weight to one side or the other and thus bring about a preponderance of power against Germany or France. The Locarno balance was not a balance of equilibrium but one of preponderance, in which the holder of the balance could decide where the preponderance lay. It was as a holder of the balance that Britain played the role of a broker. The fate of the Locarno balance depended upon how she interpreted that role in the 1930's.

Chapter Three

The Collapse
of the Balance
in the 1930's

The question that faced the statesmen of Britain and France during the 1930's was what changes in the balance of power were required to meet the new conditions of that era. Could Locarno be modified in such a way that it would continue to be an effective balance? Or, would a new balance be required in order to prevent the unlimited expansion of a new type of political movement? As we saw in Chapter One, the problem is of importance to the student of international relations because the revolutionary changes that were occurring in Western society demonstrate the difficulties of trying to use the balance of power as a means of limiting the impact of such changes on international relations.

In order to examine the problem Britain and France faced in dealing with Nazi Germany, it is first necessary to consider the *extent* and *degree* to which the balance became unbalanced as a result of the resurgence of German military power. To say that the balance "failed," or that it broke down because Germany became dominant, is not exact enough, because some measure must be made of German military dominance. Such a measure, rough though it may be, will make it possible to understand what Hitler,

Britain, and France could and could not do in the realm of international affairs. The facts of military power established constraints on Hitler as well as on Britain and France and also provided opportunities for Britain and France as well as for Hitler.

The Military Overthrow of the Locarno Balance: May 1940

One way of measuring the changes that had taken place since 1925 in the relative power positions of Britain and France and of Germany is to analyze the military balance of power at the exact point when the 1925 balance was finally demolished and Germany was at her height. How strong was Germany, in fact, when she defeated these two states in May 1940 and dominated Western Europe?

Clearly, the balance of 1925 was being eroded with increasing rapidity throughout the 1930's, and with the Hitler-Stalin Pact of 1939 it received a devastating blow from which recovery was almost impossible. To try to pinpoint the exact moment at which this balance—or any balance, for that matter—collapses is manifestly to introduce distortion into reality. Yet whatever the preceding events may tell, the point of ultimate collapse did not occur until the British and French failed to defend themselves against the German attack of May 1940, for it was then that the purpose of Locarno—to protect France against a defeat by Germany—could no longer be achieved. In May 1940 Hitler's troops, having conquered Poland, and with Eastern Europe at their feet, turned on France and destroyed her military power and her existence as an independent state; the final breakdown of the Locarno balance on the battlefields of France then became manifest for all to see. Until that month German military power had not realized itself; indeed, even the German military leaders did not know the full extent of their power, and Hitler himself had doubts. As late as the Munich crisis in September 1938, it was assumed by the British and French and by some Germans that although German power had grown to a startling degree, the overt expression of this power would be limited to German economic or quasi-military domination over Eastern Europe. Certainly, the idea that Germany could completely destroy the 1925 balance through the military defeat of France was not in their minds. Before May 1940 neither the Allies nor the German General Staff thought such a total destruction of the 1925 balance was in fact possible. Indeed, it required the full exertion of Hitler's lashing and driving will to force the German generals into an attack in the West after the defeat of Poland.

This failure to forecast what happened is usually ascribed to credulity and naiveté. But the astonishing military feat of the German Army may be a misleading guide to the actual military balance that existed even as late as May 1940. An analysis of the reasons for that victory, including the mistakes made by the Allies in military strategy, may lead to the conclusion that the balance of power was much more evenly distributed than this particular campaign indicates. If this is true, it would be a serious mistake to analyze the diplomacy of the 1930's on the assumption that Britain and France were as militarily weak as their crushing defeat of May 1940 seems to indicate and that because they were hopelessly outclassed and overweighted by German military power, they, therefore, had no means of coercing Hitler. If military power was more evenly distributed than the events of May 1940, the point of Hitler's greatest strength, seem to indicate, on the surface then both the Allied foreign policy and that of Hitler in the 1930's may be more accurately analyzed in terms of a relative equilibrium of power rather than in terms of a preponderance of power in favor of Hitler. This analysis will enable us to examine the problem of how to maintain a balance in a situation of equilibrium and also the problem faced by Hitler in trying to overthrow the balance without a preponderance of power.

Germany started the war with Poland with overwhelming military forces in respect to the Polish Army, but not with overwhelming forces if the total involvement of the German Army is to be taken into consideration. The fact that a world war was under way, therefore, made it imperative that the Polish campaign be quickly concluded. On September 1, 1939 Germany mobilized 105 divisions, including 6 Panzer, 4 light-armored, 4 motorized, 3 mountain, and 88 infantry; in addition there were 18 divisions in reserve. But of the 88 infantry divisions only 35 were formations of the Regular Army and of high quality; the remainder were suitable only for follow-up or positional warfare.[1] Against this force Poland had 30 active divisions, 10 reserve infantry divisions, 11 horsed cavalry, and 1 armored brigade; she possessed equipment reserves adequate for outfitting a total of 40 divisions but only for three months. When Germany attacked, she used 54 divisions against Poland at the very beginning, including all of her armored divisions, and two thirds of her regular and best infantry divisions; 1,600 planes were used. On September 17, the Soviet Union invaded Poland with about 20 divisions.[2]

Germany was taking no chances that the war against Poland would be anything but a short war, yet it is an interesting speculation to consider that if Stalin had been a real Machiavellian and had thrown his 20 divisions against Germany instead of Poland, and if Britain and France had immediately launched an attack on Germany from the West, as the Poles desperately begged them to do, Germany would have been hard pressed to defend herself, let alone launch an attack on France. It is manifest that

[1] J. R. M. Butler, *Grand Strategy, September 1939–June 1941* (London: 1957, United Kingdom History of the Second World War: Military series: Grand Strategy: Vol. 2), Vol. II, p. 50.
[2] *Ibid.*, pp. 54–55, 57–58.

German military power was far from dominant, in view of the possible combinations of enemies facing her, and that what carried the day was Hitler's political preparations and the political failures of his enemies. He was maneuvering on very thin military ice, even in this highly successful war, and was using a weapon that was decidedly limited in what it could achieve.

Hitler's strategy was based, therefore, on the assumption and hope that the Allies would wait for him to conclude the war in Poland and be attacked. The Allies were most cooperative. As a result, Hitler swiftly moved his troops westward after the defeat of Poland. On September 3, 1939 there were 33 German divisions in the Siegfried line; by September 21 there were 46; by December, well after the battle for Poland was concluded, there were 89.[3] The strategy of the Allies, on the other hand, was predicated on a defensive posture along the western frontier of Germany, not only because the French had already created the Maginot line, but also because the Germans had created the Siegfried line; thus, a French attack would have been costly in terms of manpower even if it had been successful. The Allies, therefore, instead of attacking during this period, held their troops ready for the purpose of moving into Belgium to meet any German thrust into northern France, where the Maginot line did not exist and the French border was open. Rather than expend their manpower in an offensive to help Poland, an effort that would probably have been futile without the cooperation of the Soviet Union, the Allies preferred to use the time granted to them by Polish resistance to build up their defense in the West. It was assumed that, if the defense of the West was feasible, German military power could be confined to Eastern Europe.

Thus, the Allies allowed the Germans to develop their plans, deploy their troops from the East to the West, and

[3] *Ibid.*, pp. 11, 60–61.

choose their own time of attack, for what seemed to them to be a logical reason. By May 1940 Germany had its troops in position. Army Group B facing Belgium and Holland had 28 divisions (3 armored, 1 motorized); Army Group A facing what was to be the crucial Ardennes sector had 44 divisions (7 armored, 3 motorized); and Army Group C facing the inactive Maginot line had 17 divisions. In addition the German Army Command (O.K.H.) possessed a reserve of 45 divisions (1 motorized) to throw in at crucial spots and for the exploitation of favorable situations. The whole totaled 134 divisions. Against this force the Allies on May 10 disposed of an almost equal number of divisions, which, considering that the offensive force must always have a considerable edge in numbers, gave them some reason for confidence. There were 22 Belgian divisions, 10 British divisions, 1 Polish division, 8 Dutch divisions, and 94 French divisions in the West, totaling 135 divisions. However, there were weaknesses in this force. Not only was it composed of disparate commands, but there had been no meaningful staff talks with Belgium and Holland despite the fact that the Allies' plan of defense was absolutely dependent on an advance into Belgium to meet the expected main German thrust through that area. In addition the Allied forces were not nearly as effective as the total figures would indicate. Of the 94 French divisions only 67 were available for use in the field; the rest were confined to the Maginot line and were trained as fortress troops. Further, the Allies had only 3 fully armored and 3 light mechanized divisions among them. While both the Germans and the French each possessed about the same number of tanks, 2,500 each, the French had them scattered throughout various divisions as support forces rather than tank (panzer) units, thus losing the great advantages that could result from concentration.

The Allies were at their weakest in the air. The French air force was composed of 549 fighters (131 of which were of an older variety) and 186 bombers, all of them obsolete.

The Germans had about 3,600 operational first-line aircraft, of which 1,180 were long-distance bombers and 366 were dive bombers. The RAF had 536 bombers and 608 fighters.[4] While German air power was superior to the Allies in both numbers and quality, this superiority was heightened by the way in which the Germans used air power in close conjunction with their land forces. The French and British air forces fought valiantly, but Germany had command of the air at all times during the May campaign and used it effectively to further the progress of her troops on the ground either through parachute drops, bombings of communication networks, terroristic dive bombing attacks, or the prevention of Allied air attacks on her land forces. The importance of this air superiority can be seen in a British Chief of Staff estimate made in early May before the actual launching of the attack of May 10. At that time the Allies believed that the Germans had 160 divisions in the West exclusive of fortress troops—a gross overestimate—as against the French and British total of 104 divisions. Yet it was thought that France should be "reasonably secure, even with this disparity, against land attack by Germany and Italy" if adequate air defense was achieved.[5]

It was not, however, mere numbers, or the quality of the troops, or even inadequate air power on the part of the Allies that brought about the collapse of May 1940. Certainly, the German General Staff and even Hitler had no illusions that they could sweep through the Allied forces, or that the latter could not stand up against the German attack. German success resulted from the adoption of a brilliant strategy, which solved the dangerous military problem facing Germany. Given the idea of an offensive against France, both Hitler and the German General Staff feared

[4] The above figures are taken from *ibid.*, pp. 33–34, 177; and L. F. Ellis, *The War in France and Flanders, 1939–1940* (London: 1953, United Kingdom History of the Second World War: Military series: Campaigns: Vol. 2), pp. 25, 44.
[5] Butler, *op. cit.*, pp. 172–173.

that an attack with the main weight thrown against Belgium would grind to a halt against the mass of Allied troops and lead to a repetition of the positional warfare of 1914–1919. This possibility haunted Hitler as a very real nightmare, and he was determined to avoid it at all costs, since such a war was precisely the kind Germany could not win. Indeed, he was a fanatic on the question of avoiding the mistake of World War I—with good reason—and he saw his particular genius, or at least one aspect of his genius, as capable of finding the answer to the problem. Thus, he as well as his generals recognized that even with the many advantages they possessed, victory in their sense of the term was not a foregone conclusion and that an attack on the West might well fail to overthrow French and British military power even if it made significant territorial gains. Yet, it was the destruction of French and British military power that was necessary. For without that destruction a long war would be forced on Germany, and as Hitler himself said to his generals, "Time is more likely to be an ally of the Western powers than of us." [6]

Yet, how was he to resolve the problem of avoiding a frontal attack on the massed Allied forces? So desperate was Hitler's situation that at first he was willing to take the chance of a direct frontal attack through Belgium. He was caught in a cleft stick, for not to make such an attack was to give the Allies time, yet if it were made, it could lead the German Army into the mud and muck of Flanders once again. He was rescued from the necessity of using a dangerous and far from certain strategy by the development in late 1939 and early 1940 of the Ardennes strategy. This plan, in large part developed by General von Manstein,[7] put the greatest German weight on the weakest sector of the Allied front and also took advantage of surprise

[6] Quoted in H. R. Trevor-Roper, ed., *Blitzkrieg to Defeat* (New York, 1965), p. 13.
[7] For his version of the plan and its origins, see E. von Manstein, *Lost Victories* (Chicago, 1958), Chs. 4, 5.

and an unexpected maneuver. It was a plan designed not simply to destroy the French and British armies but to do so quickly, although no one foresaw how quickly it was to be done in fact. The Manstein plan was not finally adopted until early 1940 over the objections of the German High Command (O.K.W.). It provided for an attack with the full weight of German armor, both tanks and motorized divisions, through the Ardennes at the hinge where Allied troop dispositions linked up with the end of the Maginot line, and that was the pivot on which the Allies would swing into Belgium. This crucial flank attack would be made by Group Army A, while Group Army B would be driving into Belgium to draw the Allies into that area, the latter assuming that Group Army B was the main threat. Thus, the encirclement of the Allied forces could be achieved. And so it worked out. When the attack was launched on May 10, the Allies, operating according to their previous plans, moved their troops into Belgium to stop what they assumed was the main thrust of the German armed forces. They walked into the trap with results that are only too well known.

This brief summary of the final collapse of the balance of 1925, in May 1940, on the field of military conflict makes it possible to identify the vital decisions and mistakes that led to the collapse, to ask why those decisions and mistakes were made and how they bear on that collapse.

The crucial decision on the Allied side was their choice of a strategy made well before the war broke out and based on the fundamental equation of Locarno; namely, that the British would come to the aid of the French in the West, but that there would be no offensive action to sustain French power or the allies of France in the East. The impact of this choice can be seen in the British concept of their military role in Europe as late as April 1938. In that month the British stated that their contribution to any coming struggle with Germany should consist mainly of naval and air forces and that Britain should not send a large army to the Continent but rather confine the army to home defense and to the defense of British territories overseas. Thus, a field force of five divisions was to be equipped for imperial defense and not for war against the Germans, while the Territorial (i.e., Reserve) units were only to be supplied with training equipment.[8] It was only in the last few months of peace (February 1939) that it was decided that even a part of the Regular Army should be equipped for the specific purpose of dealing with German military power. Even in March 1939, the month Hitler moved into Prague, the French were told by the British that while the latter would send two armored divisions to France in case of German attack, they could not arrive before September 1940. An abrupt about-face occurred, however, in April of 1939, when the British Government accepted a program that called for an eventual British army of 32 divisions, 16 of which would be sent to France in the first year of war. Conscription was introduced on April 27, and further goals were laid down for an army of 55 divisions by September 1941. This program did not indicate any basic change in British strategy, however, since it continued to postulate the "Locarno strategy," although in more effective form. If the British had had time to carry it out, the "Locarno strategy" probably would have worked. But equipment was so short in Britain at this time that when war actually did break out in 1939 not one division went to France with its full complement of equipment.

These plans, taken in conjunction with the earlier discussion of the military situation in May 1940, indicate that the "Locarno strategy" was not necessarily an incorrect decision as such, that a defensive strategy in the West could have functioned at the right time. They indicate that Hitler was correct when he said that time was on the side of the French and British, since the realization of the British troop and equipment program of April 1939

[8] Ellis, *op. cit.*, p. 2.

would probably have stymied German military power. The very idea of a blitzkrieg was born from the military weakness of Germany over the long run and from the need to prevent Britain and France from realizing their potential power. Hence, the imperative need of Hitler to destroy at least French power in 1940, since Hitler's overthrow of the 1925 balance in Eastern Europe could not be assured or completed until he had destroyed the ability of France and Britain to bring their potential power into being. But that aim could only be achieved through precise timing and meticulous strategy.

What can be said of the military situation of May 1940 can also be said of the military situation of 1938 during the Sudeten crisis. One authority contends that

. . . in September, 1938, the combined Anglo-French and Czech forces were probably qualitatively as well as quantitatively superior to the German ground forces. In fact, as late as May, 1940, the Anglo-French and German ground forces were virtually equal with respect to the quantity of war material available for combat. Qualitatively, Anglo-French material was inferior to that of Germany only in certain types of tanks. But, on the other hand, French anti-tank guns were superior to German anti-tank weapons. The Luftwaffe, of course, was superior to the Anglo-French and Czech air forces even in 1938 and by 1940 it had increased its superiority to about a three to one margin over the British and French air forces. . . . All of this does not suggest that the German military machine was not formidable in September, 1938. Rather, it does illustrate the fact that German and *"Entente"* military capabilities were virtually comparable during the *Sudeten* crisis.[9]

Kenneth Eubank in his study of the Munich crisis essentially concurs:

[9] A. H. Furnia, *The Diplomacy of Appeasement: Anglo-French Relations and the Prelude to World War II, 1931–1938* (Washington, D.C., 1960), p. 414.

After the occupation of Prague, the British army undertook to prepare thirty-two divisions—a force comparable in size to the Czechoslovak army which had been surrendered to Hitler without a fight. If Hitler had been faced in 1938 with thirty-two British divisions, thirty-five Czech divisions, and over one hundred French divisions, prepared to drive through Germany with all their strength, protected by a mighty air armada, there would not have been a Munich Agreement.[10]

Both also agree that the adoption of a defensive strategy made it impossible for the Allies to prevent Hitler from expanding in Eastern Europe. While this is true, it is clear that it was not the defensive strategy as such that was at fault but the failure to build up enough military power in the West so that Germany could not effectively attack France. This goal was well within the potentiality of the Allies. If they had achieved it, Hitler would have been faced with an even more agonizing decision; namely, should he attempt military expansion in the East knowing he could not achieve security through that expansion because he could not defeat the Allies in the West? Hitler found it difficult to develop a sound strategy for attack in the West in May 1940, when there were only 10 British divisions in France; if there had been the postulated 32 divisions of the April 1939 plan, it is probable that not even the Manstein plan would have saved him.

Hitler had to attack France in May 1940 at the latest and win during that month or not at all. Such was the narrow margin on which Hitler had to make his calculations.[11] This narrow margin had several implications for

[10] K. Eubank, *Munich* (Norman, Okla., 1963), p. 283.
[11] The Manstein plan itself was, of course, an immense gamble; Liddell Hart writing in 1965 claimed that if mines had been laid before the River Meuse, or even if trees had been felled along the forest roads leading to the Meuse, the Germans could not have won; see Captain B. H. Liddell Hart, "Was Dunkirk Really Necessary?" *The Observer,* June 6, 1965. For a detailed but concise study of the May 10 attack, see J. Benoist-Méchin, *Sixty Days that Shook the West* (New York, 1963).

the foreign policies of the Allies and Germany in the years before World War II and for the ways in which the former tried to maintain the balance and in which the latter tried to overthrow it.

1. The foreign policy of Chamberlain was, in its most fundamental aspects, predicated on the military viability of the "Locarno strategy." It was the assumption that the West could stand up against Hitler that made it feasible for Chamberlain to contemplate the expansion of Germany in Eastern Europe, for if such was the case, the basic aim of the balance would be achieved, namely, the independence of France regardless of Hitler's power in the East. As we shall see, the *form* this expansion in Eastern Europe would take was of crucial importance to Chamberlain's calculations, but there is a close link between appeasement and the "Locarno strategy," for the latter made the former a tolerable and even *necessary* expedient. Chamberlain refused to contemplate a world war over the question of the Sudetenland and was determined to give the Sudetenland to Hitler because he believed it was not a vital interest of the West to force Hitler to stay his hand in Eastern Europe. It was not a vital interest because Britain and France were secured by the "Locarno strategy," at least in theory.

2. But if the "Locarno strategy" was a sound and logical basis for appeasement, the then current military weaknesses of that strategy, as Chamberlain conceived of those weaknesses, added to the reasons for adopting appeasement. Chamberlain, it is clear, overestimated German military power in the years immediately preceding the war. By doing so he saw that Britain could do little to influence events in the East until her power to defend herself *in the West* was rebuilt. Once that defensive power in the West was achieved, the effects of the "Locarno strategy" would be felt with full force by Hitler. German expansion in the East could then be controlled and limited by threatening Hitler with a general war, which he knew he could

not win in the West. But until the British were in a position
to make such a threat, appeasement was an attempt in the
diplomatic sphere to restrict and contain Hitler's eastward
expansion. While Chamberlain was at least intermittently
aware of the fallibility of such efforts, he also had great
faith that diplomatic efforts could in themselves achieve his
objectives. The importance of the fact that the decision to
expand the British military contribution to France's continental efforts was not made until *April 1939* is that not
until Hitler's takeover of Prague in March 1939 did Chamberlain see that a sudden increase in military power would
be necessary to prevent Hitler from acting unilaterally in
the East.[12] That Chamberlain would have used an effective
"Locarno strategy" to coerce Hitler to some extent, while
giving him some of the things he wanted, is virtually certain; that he thought the weaknesses of the West were such
that he could not use such coercive power in 1938 is also
virtually certain. Appeasement in the latter case, therefore,
was bound to be a different type of appeasement than in
the former case. In 1938-1939, when Chamberlain saw
the West as militarily weak, he thought he had to rely on
bargaining unsupported by coercion, even though he hoped
at the same time to come as close to the first type of appeasement as possible. The tragedy of Chamberlain's position in 1938 was that the West was in a much stronger
military position than he or his experts recognized, that
the distribution of power was much more even and Hitler's
advantages much more marginal than they seemed to be
to those making policy in the West at the time.

   3. If the "Locarno strategy" formed the basis of Chamberlain's policy, it was also the basis for Hitler's policies.
The marginality of Hitler's military advantages in the West
posed precisely the problem that Hitler had to solve. It

[12] Even after the takeover of Prague, however, Chamberlain continued to depend to some considerable extent on diplomatic appeasement; see M. Gilbert and R. Gott, *The Appeasers* (Boston,
1963), Part 3.

was in response to the fact of his precarious military advantages that the concept of a military blitzkrieg was invented, an attempt to bring about a military decision before the opponent or—more important—the allies of his opponents could mobilize. But not only was Hitler's margin of superiority small in 1938 and 1940; before then it was nonexistent, and in a strictly military sense Germany was in a position of decided inferiority. Even as late as the occupation of Austria in March 1938, the German Army was not ready for an offensive war of great magnitude. Hitler's task, therefore, was to manipulate the political forces of continental Europe in such a way that the superior military forces of other states would not be brought to bear on him. But his task was even greater than that. Given his aims, which will be discussed below, he also had to avoid the acceptance of those concessions that would require the granting of concessions by him to other states, since to do so would involve the establishment of a new balance of power and would, therefore, act as a limit on his actions. He had, thus, to avoid a new Locarno conference and any bargaining situation. For a bargaining confrontation would force him into foreign policy concessions because his military power was too weak to make it possible for him not to do so once he had accepted the principle of a bargain. To bargain on his objectives would have been to recognize limits on his foreign policy purposes, especially on his plans for the creation and use of the Wehrmacht. Hitler, therefore, put himself outside the framework of diplomatic exchange and even rejected offers to change the Locarno status quo for a new status quo, because even a new status quo, if attained through diplomatic bargaining, would achieve less than he wanted and would not bolster his weak military position to the degree he desired. Hitler's methods, his refusal of diplomacy, were in part dictated by military weakness rather than military strength. As we shall see, Hitler constantly engaged in a pretense of concessions—"this is my last territorial claim"

was the usual refrain that followed an act of expansion—
but in fact he avoided of necessity any concrete reorganization of the balance, even when Germany could have
benefited. It was not until late 1938, when his military
position was about to reach its peak, that he dared face
the prospect of a large-scale conference of the Locarno
Powers. Even then he rejected negotiation and simply used
diplomacy as a way of making demands without accepting
any. Hitler's aims, combined with the fact of military
weakness, made it imperative for him to avoid real negotiation and concessions because they would lead to restrictions on the power of the German armed forces. This,
then, was a situation in which a weaker power, which desired to expand, refused concessions from the stronger
powers; it was a complete reversal of Stresemann's position.

4. It is clear that the strictly military balance in the
years 1938–1940 was so close to an equilibrium that a
relatively minor decision about tactics, a decision that
might be called "technical," could cause the breakdown of
the balance. The "technical" decision in this case was General Manstein's tactical plan of striking through the Ardennes area rather than through Belgium. The instability of
the balance derived in large part from this condition of
near-equilibrium. In these circumstances manipulation of
the balance of power in order to maintain the balance was
an extremely difficult and complex task for Britain and
France because the narrow range of the differences between the Allies and Germany made it both tempting and
possible for Germany to believe that a "technical" decision
could act as the decisive extra ounce of power that would
destroy the whole apparatus. Hence, it was difficult for
Chamberlain to bring to bear whatever coercive power
Britain possessed because Hitler thought a "technical" decision would enable him to escape from the impact of such
coercion. Does such a conclusion indicate that equilibrium,
or near-equilibrium, situations are inherently unstable? No,

because a leader other than Hitler might not have used the opportunities offered by an equilibrium precisely because the chances were too risky. There is every evidence that the German General Staff would have refused the risks taken by Hitler. Any conclusions about the stability and instability of a situation of equilibrium must take into account, therefore, the willingness of the leadership of the various states involved in a balance to play the role of broker and to seek changes and modifications in the balance through brokerage. To understand the problems faced by those who wished to maintain the balance of power in the 1930's it is necessary to consider the nature of Hitler's aims and methods and the problems they posed for the brokerage process. We will then be in a position to study the ways in which Chamberlain tried to modify Hitler's policies in order to preserve the balance.

Hitler's Intentions and Diplomacy

After World War II broke out and even after Munich, it was widely assumed that the failure of the British and French to protect themselves against Hitler was due to ignorance, mental blindness, and refusal to face the facts of Hitler's intentions, which were perfectly clear to anyone who wished to understand them. The problem this conclusion presented to the student of international relations, therefore, was not that of attempting to understand and analyze Hitler's motives, but rather of endeavoring to understand why Britain and France failed to comprehend them. Obviously, such an analysis is still pertinent. Given Hitler's objectives, one of the crucial issues this era presents is why British and French statesmen failed to manipulate the political situation in such a way that the balance could be maintained. Yet even that problem cannot be accurately understood without knowing not only what Hitler intended but also the methods he used to attain his ends. For the methods would in practice modify the ends, and if the British and French could influence his methods sufficiently to maintain the balance, the "ultimate" or long-range ends of Hitler would cease to be of much significance.

Since the end of the war, the appearance of documentation on the prewar period and a willingness to reexamine the evidence in a more dispassionate frame of mind have made it possible to raise questions concerning Hitler's actions and to describe them with more accuracy. This reexamination has not greatly changed the picture of Hitler as an aggressive and brutal leader determined to use German power to the fullest in Europe. But it has added complexities and made the question of the relationship between Hitler's large-scale dreams and his day-to-day opportunism less simple than it once seemed; certainly, it is clear that it cannot be claimed that a "plan" for the "conquest" of Europe or for a world war existed except in the most vague and general sense that such plans always exist in the mind of such a leader. The once popular idea that *Mein Kampf* stated Hitler's "plans" and that *Mein Kampf* was, so to speak, the beginning and end of Hitler's foreign policy is no longer sufficient. As one authority puts it: "In the course of time . . . the circumstances in which Hitler tried to realize his ideas as well as those ideas themselves, changed, and hence *Mein Kampf* gradually loses value as the criterion for testing Hitler's political principles." [13]

To be sure, *Mein Kampf* is still an invaluable guide to the junk heap of ideas that was Hitler's mind, and for the student of international relations it is a useful guide to the ways in which the Nazi movement looked upon the map of Europe. It also tells a great deal about the ways in which traditional German views of the German position in Europe and especially Eastern Europe were distorted and manipulated to form the basis of the Nazi ideology. Germany had always had an ambitious policy in Eastern Europe and

[13] E. M. Robertson, *Hitler's Pre-War Policy and Military Plans, 1933–1939* (London, 1963), p. 2.

had always seen the area as one that "belonged" to her in one form or another. In the hands of most German leaders this attitude meant a sphere of German influence. As we have seen, Stresemann essentially held this view, although in more temperate form than some of his contemporaries, such as General von Seeckt, for example. In *Mein Kampf* Hitler took this general orientation and expanded it into a full-blown and grandiose scheme for acquiring "new soil" to which the "superfluous millions" of Germans could be sent each year.[14] In his view,

Such a territorial policy cannot be fulfilled in the Cameroons, but today almost exclusively in Europe. We must, therefore, coolly and objectively adopt the standpoint that it can certainly not be the intention of Heaven to give one people fifty times as much land and soil in this world as another. In this case we must not let political boundaries obscure for us the boundaries of eternal justice. If this earth really has room for all to live in, let us be given the soil we need for our livelihood.

True, they [sic] will not willingly do this. But then the law of self-preservation goes into effect; and what is refused to amicable methods, it is up to the fist to take. If our forefathers had let their decisions depend on the same pacifistic nonsense as our contemporaries, we should possess only a third of our present territory; but in that case there would scarcely be any German people for us to worry about in Europe today. No—it is our natural determination to fight for our own existence that we owe the two *Ostmarks* of the Reich and hence that inner strength arising from the greatness of our state and national territory which alone has enabled us to exist up to the present.[15]

This type of hortatory prose is less impressive as a guide to Hitler's foreign policy than it looks, and poses more questions than it answers. Not only is it carefully vague in

[14] A. Hitler, *Mein Kampf*, trans. R. Manheim (Sentry ed., Boston, 1943), p. 137.
[15] *Ibid.*, pp. 138–139.

its prescription and not only were such trashy thoughts widespread in Germany at that time, but to accept such statements as a guide to Hitler's actions when he came to power would be to assume a one-to-one relationship between a leader's words and his acts, a proposition manifestly incorrect in the case of other leaders and no less so in the case of Hitler. Indeed, the very problem Hitler posed to the leaders of other states was exactly what relationship would exist between his words and his acts when he came to power. It is not to be denied that *Mein Kampf* should have alerted anyone to the fact that Hitler was an advocate of a ruthless expansion of German power *beyond* the pre-1914 frontiers of Germany in contradistinction to even the most ardent followers of the German right-wing conservative parties, who mainly wished to restore to Germany those territories lost by the peace of 1919. No one can have any doubt that Hitler intended, both before and after he came to power, to destroy the particular balance of power as it was established at Locarno, and to destroy it in such a way that there would be German preponderance in Europe. But one might legitimately have considerable doubts about the extent and form that German expansion would take under Hitler in practice when he was face-to-face with the realities of foreign policy. Hitler's words could not, *taken in and of themselves,* tell how he would conduct his foreign policy.

However lurid Hitler's dreams of power might be, the facts of international life would force him to adopt a position one way or another toward what was happening around him and thereby immediately introduce a major modification into his simplistic, not to say simpleminded, image of what he was going to do in the real world. Indeed, it was part of Hitler's genius that he was able to mediate so effectively between the half-mad world of his dreams (which he retailed to his audiences in Germany) and the realities of foreign policy and to somehow bring the two together. The realities of foreign policy were far different from the realities of domestic politics; Hitler could not as easily gun down his opponents in foreign affairs as he did his foes inside Germany in the bloodbath of June 30, 1934. What the record shows is not a resolute Hitler marching irrevocably forward in pursuit of his foreordained and already enunciated plans but an irresolute Hitler improvising to use every opportunity to expand German power and forced to tailor his ends to his limited means. W. N. Medlicott puts Hitler's problem clearly: "The problem of ways and means was . . . at once emotional, diplomatic, and strategical. We can detect a conflict, mainly unconscious perhaps, between his lust for great military victories and his canny desire to gain the hegemony of Europe as economically as possible." [16]

None of this is to ignore the fact that Hitler was preparing for war. But the crucial question was, what kind of war, where, and when? As the previous discussion of the military balance in 1940 has shown, Hitler's military means were decidedly limited. While the precise extent of the limits varied over the years 1933–1939 and while Hitler by 1938 had clearly re-created the German armed forces and restored German military power to a position of strength, at no time was Hitler in possession of a force that was so dominant that he did not have to calculate carefully the power and intent of his opponents. The closeness of the limits within which he had to work is shown not only by the amount of military power at his disposal but also by the economic resources and planning of the Third Reich. Recent studies of the German economy show that the assumption made in the 1930's that Hitler was creating a total war economy, which was fully devoted to the making of the tools of war, was not true. The

[16] W. N. Medlicott, "The Coming of War in 1939," in W. N. Medlicott, ed., *From Metternich to Hitler: Aspects of British and Foreign History, 1814–1939* (New York, 1963), p. 239.

German economy was never organized for the production
of war goods on the largest possible scale until the very
end of the war. Certainly, the Nazi government was preparing for war, but an "inspection of Germany's prewar
pattern of investment shows that there was no pronounced
concentration of investment in those activities associated
with economic preparations for war." [17] The same authority goes on to comment that in the prewar period "an
enormous diversion of resources from the civilian to the
war sector of the economy did not occur." [18] He concludes:

The volume of expenditures for rearmament (in the prewar period) was actually quite modest. In the period 1933
through 1938 rearmament expenditure absorbed less than
10 per cent of Germany's gross national product, and even
as late as 1938, only 15 per cent. . . . Whether we examine the general nature of the German economic recovery,
or the raw material self-sufficiency program, or the mobilization of manpower, the same general conclusion is evident: The scale of Germany's economic mobilization for
war was quite modest.[19]

One result of this limited rearmament program was that in
the autumn of 1939 German aircraft production was no
more than that of Great Britain and her tank production
was smaller.[20]

Obviously, by 1939 the scale of German rearmament
was such that it had acquired a larger backlog of weapons
and arms than had Britain and France. But the German
war machine, in both its military and economic aspects,
was designed for short, limited wars, for blitzkriegs against
weak opponents who were fighting alone, and not for all-
out, total war against an alliance of large powers. As a re-

[17] B. H. Klein, *Germany's Economic Preparations for War* (Cambridge, Mass.), p. 15.
[18] *Ibid.*, p. 16.
[19] *Ibid.*, pp. 76, 78. A. S. Milward in *The German War Economy*
(London, 1965) comes to fundamentally the same conclusions.
[20] Klein, *op. cit.*, pp. 3–4.

sult, Hitler had to choose carefully the place, the means, and the time for the expansion of German power beyond the borders of Germany. It does not follow that Hitler did not intend to go to war; but it does follow that he had to move in such a way that the forces of the existing balance of power should not be united and brought to bear on him. Yet his aims were such that he also had to take the risk of doing exactly that, of uniting those forces and bringing them into operation in order to preserve the balance.

It is in relationship to this combination of caution made necessary by the limits of his actual power and risk made necessary by his wide-ranging aims that the course of Hitler's foreign policy should be analyzed. Hitler's first move after breaking off relations with the League of Nations and discontinuing disarmament negotiations was to safeguard his eastern frontier by a nonaggression pact with Poland in 1934, a move calculated to astonish the chancelleries of Europe in view of German passion concerning the territory "lost" to Poland. But in acting to weaken the French alliance system in Eastern Europe, Hitler was in a position to make his first significant frontal attack on the balance of power through the rearmament of Germany.

Thus, Hitler's second step in restoring German power was the announcement on March 16, 1935 of the unilateral rearmament of Germany. This effort to establish a military basis for Hitler's plans, in open defiance of the Versailles Treaty, brought about an immediate reaction from other powers. At a meeting of Britain, France, and Italy at Stresa, April 11–14, 1935, the so-called Stresa Front came into being as a group of states opposed to Hitler's action. It was potentially an alliance of the three states against Germany, for at Stresa they not only stated their opposition to the unilateral rearmament of Germany but also reaffirmed the Locarno Treaties. There were other reactions. At Geneva the League of Nations condemned the German action. France and Russia drew together for the first time since the war through the signing of a mutual assistance pact on May 2, 1935; Franco-Italian agreements of military cooperation on land and in the air against Germany had already been signed in January 1935. A Czech-Soviet rapprochement began. Hitler's action had clearly called into being an encircling network of alliances and agreements directed specifically against Germany.[21] But the network was more fictitious than real. Before the British had gone to Stresa, they had gone to Berlin to talk with Hitler in order to promote what they called a "general understanding," despite Hitler's announcement of the rearmament of Germany; the French made no real effort to give substance to the Franco-Soviet agreement;[22] and finally, the shadow of the coming Italo-Ethiopian war was already being cast on the relations of Italy with Britain and France. It was to be a war, that, in combination with Italian intervention in the Spanish Civil War, would cause tension between Britain and France and throw Italy into a dependent relationship with Germany, thus preventing Italy from applying effective power in European affairs.[23]

These reactions against Hitler's rearmament of Germany were a significant effort to bring the balance of power into action against Hitler. This was especially true of the Franco-Soviet mutual assistance pact. It has been said that

. . . the origins of the Franco-Soviet Pact of Mutual Assistance present an almost classical display of balance-of-power diplomacy . . . the balance of power was moving in precise and logical grooves. The aggressor had appeared, he had frightened his victims, and they had dropped their own quarrels to cling together.[24]

[21] For an excellent account of European diplomacy in the years 1933–1935, see W. E. Scott, *Alliance Against Hitler: The Origins of the Franco-Soviet Pact* (Durham, N.C., 1962).
[22] *Ibid.*, Ch. 12.
[23] See *Documents on German Foreign Policy, 1918–1945* (Washington, D.C., 1949 ff.), Ser. C, Vol. IV, Doc. 87: Hereafter cited as DGFP.
[24] Scott, *op. cit.*, pp. 256, 267.

THE COLLAPSE OF THE BALANCE 135

The same author, however, makes it clear the system eventually failed to cohere. Yet, in the spring of 1935 this failure was still in the future. Hitler was still operating from a position of great weakness. He had announced that with the expansion of the German Army under the action taken on March 16, it would be comprised of 36 divisions (600,000 troops). This was impressive when it is considered that the French Army in metropolitan France was only 405,000 troops. It became less impressive if the British Army of 154,000 troops and the Italian Army of 600,000 to 800,000 troops were added to the French. It became even less impressive if it is realized that the 36 divisions were nowhere in sight and that by March 1936 the German Army possessed not 36 divisions but 25 full-strength divisions and had a total of about 500,000 troops, the same as the French Army, which had expanded in the meantime.[25] Certainly, the German armed forces were suddenly powerful after the long night of the Versailles restrictions; but it is equally certain that they were not capable of offensive action at this time, especially not against the Stresa Front or the Franco-Soviet alliance.

Hitler's answer to his encirclement was to use diplomacy to break the ring. In a major speech, which followed the Franco-Soviet pact by nineteen days, he offered the possibility of negotiation on the issues outstanding between Germany and the rest of Europe. But while it was directed to Europe as a whole,[26] it was especially directed to the British, who were, as the British Foreign Secretary Sir John Simon said to the German Ambassador on May 10, 1935, hoping "for a positive statement of the German position." They got it. And they reacted positively themselves to Hitler's assertion that under certain circumstances Germany would reenter the League of Nations, that he would

[25] The above figures are taken from Scott, *op. cit.,* p. 231, n. 24; Klein, *op. cit.,* p. 17; and Robertson, *op. cit.,* p. 83.
[26] The major portion of this speech can be found in DGFP, Ser. C, Vol. IV, Doc. 102.

respect the Versailles Treaty other than the section on disarmament, and that he was willing to consider an air pact[27]
with the Western powers, an Eastern pact of nonaggression
with the states of Eastern Europe, as well as arms, including naval, limitations. The British were especially interested
in negotiating an air pact and in holding naval conversations as soon as possible.[28] The result was one of Hitler's
masterpieces, the Anglo-German Naval Pact (signed June
18, 1935), which provided that Germany would limit her
navy to 35 percent of the British navy. The German motives in negotiating the pact were several. First, they wished
to mollify the British by refusing to engage in naval competition with them and hence to avoid the error of the pre-
1914 years. In addition the pact would split Britain from
France, a calculation that worked to a nicety, since only
two months after Stresa Britain was seen publicly to desert
France and to make a separate agreement with Germany.[29]
An unsigned memorandum of the German Foreign Min-
istry summed up the advantages of the pact for Germany.
After pointing out that even if they wanted to do so, the
Germans could not build more ships than the proportion
allowed under the treaty, it went on:

The success of the Agreement lies principally in the political sphere. In this respect its consequences should not be
underrated. As a result of the Agreement the most powerful
of our former enemies and of the signatories of the Versailles Treaty has formally invalidated an important part
of this Treaty and formally recognized Germany's equality
of rights. The danger of Germany's being isolated, which

[27] The air pact would have provided that the signatories would
come to the aid of any member of the group who was subjected to
unprovoked air attack. It was intended to lessen the possibility of
using air power as an offensive weapon.
[28] DGFP, Ser. C, Vol. IV, Doc. 104.
[29] For the French reaction to this agreement, see Royal Institute
of International Affairs, A. J. Toynbee, ed., *Survey of International
Affairs, 1935* (London, 1936), Vol. I.

definitely threatened in March and April of this year, has been eliminated. A political understanding with Great Britain has been initiated by the naval settlement. The front recently formed against us by the Stresa Powers has been considerably weakened by the Agreement.[30]

The reasons why the British made the agreement are to be found in the deep-seated preoccupation of British foreign policy, which will be considered below. Here it need only be said that the agreement forestalled naval competition and thus helped resolve Britain's difficult financial and strategic problems.

Hitler escaped from immediate consequences of his action in March 1935, not only by shrewd understanding of the divisions among his opponents, but by the shrewd use of negotiations to exploit those divisions when he was in a weak military position. If the Stresa Front had been not just a front but a reality, significant opposition to Germany could have been triggered off in 1935 rather than 1939. A significant coalition of powers could have come into existence to block any further moves,[31] and Hitler would have possessed few resources with which to combat it. Hence, his imperative need to move carefully and to present himself as one who wished to negotiate the problems of Europe in the Locarno manner.

A similar pattern presented itself in 1936, when Hitler reoccupied the Rhineland on March 7. Germany once again operated from a position of military weakness and this time took even greater risks than in 1935. The reoccupation of the Rhine territories involved a head-on clash with both Britain and France because it meant the end of

[30] DGFP, Ser. C, Vol. IV, Doc. 275. It is interesting to note that the agreement was faithfully carried out by the Germans until they denounced it in 1939. The above memorandum is dated August 28, 1935.
[31] Robertson, *op. cit.,* pp. 9–24, makes the point that in the first eight months after Hitler took office there was a real possibility of foreign intervention in Germany to put down the Nazi regime.

the Locarno Treaties and because it was a direct attack
on French military power. But the collision was necessary.
Hitler's task was precisely to destroy the basis of the Locarno balance and hence to achieve freedom of maneuver
in Eastern Europe through the remilitarization of the
Rhine. His action in 1936 was one of the crucial steps in
the disruption and breakdown of the 1925 balance. Yet,
when it was carried out, the strictly military balance was
still in favor of his opponents, despite the defection of
Mussolini to Hitler's side during the crisis. As we have
seen, Germany possessed no more than 25 divisions in
March 1936; there were also many problems of command,
organization, and shortages of supplies and equipment at
that date. France, Poland, and Czechoslovakia by themselves had 90 divisions in peacetime and 190 in wartime.
If one adds to these forces the divisions of the Soviet Union,
now an official ally of France,[32] and the naval and economic power of Britain, it is clear that in strictly military
terms Germany would be outclassed in case of a major
conflict. It was for this reason that the German General
Staff opposed the plan for the reoccupation of the Rhine
in 1936 and wished to postpone it until the military position
of Germany should drastically improve.[33] They assumed
that the French would not permit German troops to place
themselves once again on their frontier. Hence the attempt

[32] Obviously, one must not ignore the grave internal weaknesses of
the Soviet Union at this time, which threatened to undermine her
military potential. All that is meant here is to indicate the magnitude
of the potential facing Hitler. For information on the nature of
Soviet armed forces in this period, see J. Erickson, *The Soviet High
Command: A Military-Political History 1918–1941* (New York,
1962), Parts 4, 5.

[33] J. W. Wheeler-Bennett, *The Nemesis of Power: The German
Army in Politics, 1918–1945* (2nd ed., London, 1964), pp. 349–350.
It should be noted that there were numerous unofficial and para-
military troops under Nazi control in the Rhine before March 7.
General Gamelin on March 28, 1936 estimated those to total about
265,000 troops including 150,000 SA troops. See *Documents Diplomatiques Français, 1932–1939* (Paris, 1963 ff.), 2d ser., Vol. 1, Doc.
525, n. 1: Hereafter cited as *Doc. Diplo. Fran.*

of General von Beck to make Hitler declare that he would
not fortify the area west of the Rhine and the successful
efforts of other German generals to get a private promise
from Hitler that any troops sent across the Rhine would
be withdrawn if France should offer significant military
opposition.[34] Even Hitler was concerned about his military
situation, admitting later that "the forty-eight hours after
the march into the Rhineland were the most nerve-wrack-
ing in my whole life. . . . If the French had marched into
the Rhineland we should have had to retreat with ignominy,
for we had not the military resources at our disposal for
even a feeble resistance." [35] The weakness of the German
military position is further revealed by the fact that only
one division was moved into the Rhineland and only three
battalions across the Rhine and that when Britain and
France displayed their displeasure at the move, the German General Staff wanted to bring the three battalions back
across the Rhine.[36]

Displeasure was, however, all that the British and French
displayed. The key to the balance of power in Europe was
turned over to Germany quite literally without a shot being fired. It was an incredible moment in history and even
today one marvels at the opportunity that was lost.

Hitler took the risk that Britain and France would not
seriously contest the loss of the Rhineland because he, unlike his generals, made a political calculation rather than
a purely military one. For the political situation in Europe
was as ripe for the remilitarization of the Rhine as it would
ever be. In March 1936 the Ethiopian question was reaching its ultimate climax with the question of oil sanctions
against Italy before the League of Nations and with Italian
arms finally attaining success. If Hitler was to take advantage of the divisive effects of the Ethiopian war, he

[34] Wheeler-Bennett, *op. cit.*, p. 352. See also Robertson, *op. cit.*,
pp. 71–79.
[35] Quoted, Wheeler-Bennett, *op. cit.*, p. 353, n. 1.
[36] A. Bullock, *Hitler: A Study in Tyranny* (rev. ed., New York,
1964), p. 343.

would have to do so soon. Not only had the war thrown
Mussolini into Hitler's arms, although without great enthusiasm on the part of Mussolini,[37] but it had kept Britain
preoccupied with the Italian threat to the Mediterranean.
In a meeting of French military leaders on March 8, 1936,
which had been called to consider the Rhineland situation,
the French Admiral Duran-Viel put it plainly:

England cannot now give us anything but moral support.
It is necessary above all that the Ethiopian affair be liquidated. It is impossible to see how common action between
England and Italy can take place if they are in a state of
hostility to each other. When that hostility ceases it will
take at least 15 days before English naval forces could be
ready to act in the North Sea and the Channel. In fact the
British Isles are now without naval protection.[38]

In addition to weakening Britain vis-à-vis Germany, the
Ethiopian war had caused a deep rift between Britain and
France. Yet such rifts could easily be mended, and although the Hoare-Laval plan of December 1935 had failed
to do so, with the defeat of Ethiopia only a few months
away, their cooperation would quickly revive along with
British sea power in the North and Channel seas. Even
with the situation as it was, Anglo-French staff talks had
been under way in December 1935 and January 1936.[39]
Finally, the approval of the Franco-Soviet Pact in late
February 1936 by the Chamber of Deputies, after many
delays caused by Laval's reluctance to be closely tied to the
Soviet Union, indicated that France had finally taken the
plunge into close Franco-Soviet relations. Indeed, it was
this ratification that was the ostensible reason for the remilitarization of the Rhineland. Hitler had waited until the
last minute to make his move.

[37] See the dispatches of von Hassel, German Ambassador to Italy
for this period: DGFP, Ser. C, Vol. IV; and Robertson, op. cit., pp.
66–91.
[38] Doc. Diplo. Fran., 2d ser., Vol. 1, Doc. 334, p. 445.
[39] Robertson, op. cit., p. 69.

Although the situation in March 1936 was as favorable for Hitler's objective as it would ever be, it still contained a large element of risk for him. Not only had he waited until the last minute, and not only were the forces opposing him in the process of regrouping after the effects of the Ethiopian war, but by all the rules of balance of power politics France should have unhesitatingly opposed Hitler's march into the Rhineland with any and all the means at her disposal; as we have seen, even in Hitler's eyes those means were potent and effective. And there was every reason to believe that they would be used. But they were not used, a fact that caused the German generals to consider themselves "betrayed by their fellow military trade unionists on the other side who had not made the proper gambits and who refused to take advantage of their undoubted superiority." [40]

Why didn't the French play the game according to the rules? Why, at this crucial point, did the balance of power fail to function? The deeper causes of this failure must be left to an analysis of British and French foreign policy in the next section, but it is appropriate to consider here the military causes of this failure.

At a meeting of the French military leaders on March 8, General Gamelin stated the point of view that ultimately prevailed and that he gave as his answer to the French Government when they asked him what could be done to meet the German reoccupation. Gamelin believed that nothing short of a full-scale war would result if the French should enter into the previously demilitarized zone, that *"la guerre sera déclenchée,"* and that, accordingly, general mobilization would be necessary. He even saw the possibility of a theater of operations in Belgium and demanded that British and Italian troops come immediately to France and that France be allowed to enter into Belgium.[41] France, he

---

[40] Wheeler-Bennett, *op. cit.*, p. 353.

[41] *Doc. Diplo. Fran.*, 2d ser., Vol. 1, Doc. 334, March 8, 1936. Gamelin summarized his position thus: *"Si nous nous opposons par la force à cette occupation, c'est la guerre,"* p. 444.

claimed, would have to mobilize a force of about 1,200,000 troops: in Gamelin's opinion this force would be just barely superior to the number then serving in the German Army[42] —a gross exaggeration of German strength, as we now know. The French military leaders even foresaw German air attacks on Paris and French towns along the Rhine frontier, as well as German submarine action.[43] The Minister of the Navy supported this point of view when he pointed out to the French Government that this was not the year 1923.[44]

That the French military problem appeared to their military leadership as more complicated than might appear to outsiders was revealed by a memorandum by General Gamelin dated March 28, 1936, in which he examined what he called the problem of the "eventual penetration" of French troops into the Rhine area. Such a penetration, according to his analysis, required a French expeditionary corps that was trained and equipped for offensive strike action. But this corps did not exist. As for the occupation of the Ruhr, that could no longer be carried out as it had been in 1923. Thus, given the mobilization of 1,000,000 troops, the best he could offer was the establishment of a war front that would achieve a military equilibrium outside the borders of France and would lead to victory only after a long attrition of German power.[45] General Gamelin's admission that France could only mount a static defense and that she was, therefore, technically unprepared to meet the problem of the German remilitarization of the Rhine is an astounding admission of failure to develop the proper means to achieve the crucial foreign policy objective of France, control over the Rhineland. The source of this failure lies not only in the general nature of the French

[42] *Ibid.*, Doc. 392, March 11, 1936, p. 505.
[43] *Ibid.*
[44] *Ibid.*, Doc. 406, March 12, 1936, pp. 522–523.
[45] *Ibid.*, Doc. 525, pp. 696–700.

Army at this time[46] as a cadre for the reserves but also in the whole nature of French military planning since Locarno. After 1923 the French had increasingly come to the conclusion that what happened in Eastern Europe was important but not vital as long as the fortress itself, France, was impregnable.

The French refusal to move against Germany also resulted from the assumption that France could not act without allies. Gamelin insisted that France could act against Germany only if she had the support of a coalition, the crucial member of which would be Britain. Poland offered to act with France against the reoccupation[47] and Czechoslovakia offered to support economic and financial sanctions against Germany,[48] but Britain was the necessary partner. Thus, the French called upon Britain to support France in military action against Germany. In the light of French estimates at that time of their inability to take effective action and of their doubts about what they could achieve if they did act, it is hard to believe that they intended to do more than they did, which was simply to send thirteen divisions to man the French frontier. However, they were in no danger of having their hand forced by the British. The British Prime Minister, Stanley Baldwin, told his foreign secretary, Eden, when informed of French concern that "though personally friendly to France, he was clear in his mind that there would be no support in Britain for military action by the French." [49] Britain would also refuse to support financial and economic sanctions.[50] Instead, she wished to pursue the negotiation of an air pact with Germany and the return of Germany to the League of Nations. The most that Britain would offer France was the

[46] See E. M. Earle, ed., *Makers of Modern Strategy* (Princeton, 1941), Ch. 15.
[47] *Bullock, op. cit.,* p. 345; cf. *Doc. Diplo. Fran., op. cit.,* Doc. 303.
[48] *Doc Diplo. Fran., op. cit.,* Docs. 343, 344, 402.
[49] A. Eden, *Facing the Dictators* (Boston, 1962), p. 385.
[50] *Ibid.,* p. 388.

staff talks, which began on April 15, 1936.[51] The military basis of her refusal to act was not unlike that of France, since the British Chiefs of Staff had reported on March 12 that mobilization and the withdrawal of British forces from the Mediterranean, where "all our efficient war materiel was concentrated," would be necessary if action was to be taken against Hitler.[52]

Once again Hitler acted and then offered negotiations in order to divide those opposing him.[53] To replace Locarno, he suggested a twenty-five-year nonaggression pact to France and Belgium as well as the air pact, in which Britain was especially interested; Britain and Italy were again to act as guarantors of the nonaggression pact. He also offered nonaggression pacts to the states of Eastern Europe, to bring Germany back to the League of Nations, and the demilitarization of both sides of the Franco-German border. Both France and Britain, but especially France, were cool to these proposals. Nothing came of them because the British insisted that any nonaggression pact in the West provide for arrangements for mutual aid between Britain, France, and Belgium.[54] Thus, Britain attempted to square the circle by offering to discuss Hitler's proposals, but only within the framework of automatic military plans with France against Germany.

Despite the weakness of the French and British response, the results of the reoccupation of the Rhineland could not have been completely pleasing to Hitler, for the British determination to fight for and at the side of France was strengthened as a result of his blow at French power. And even though the British determination was not adequate to prevent Hitler from building up his power in Eastern Europe, he nevertheless moved cautiously and with a sense of

[51] *Ibid.*, p. 417.
[52] *Ibid.*, p. 400.
[53] Robertson, *op. cit.*, pp. 80–81.
[54] Eden, *op. cit.*, p. 403.

the limits of German power, even in view of the fact that
France had lost her ability to fight for Eastern Europe
since German reoccupation of the Rhineland. The occupation of Austria in March 1938—always the month of
March!—waited two years. Hitler hoped to avoid the use
of military force and an open military occupation of Austria. Rather, he planned that a process of gradual internal
change would make Austria a sort of satellite of Germany.
Thus a clear confrontation with the West would be avoided;
German military power would be used for no more than a
tacit support for internal change.[55] (Indeed, it seems that
it was not until German troops had actually moved into
Austria and Hitler had appeared as a returning hero in his
hometown of Linz that he became intoxicated with his
success and decided to make Austria a part of Germany
proper.)[56] And even to achieve a process of gradual internal
change, Hitler had to reckon with Mussolini, who in 1934
had moved his troops up to the Austrian border in order to
prevent a Nazi takeover after the murder of Dollfuss. But
by 1938 Mussolini had allowed himself once again to be
embroiled in a long-drawn-out military campaign, this
time in Spain, in his madcap search for hegemony in the
Mediterranean. The result was once again to bring Britain
and Italy into conflict and to weaken their abilities to react
against the movements of Hitler. Yet, even though Mussolini was in no position to protect Austrian independence,
Hitler almost exploded with relief when he learned that
Mussolini would now play a passive role in this area. The
record of the telephone conversation in which Prince Philip
of Hesse, the German Ambassador to Italy, told the news
to Hitler is worthy of quotation.

[55] G. Brook-Shepard, *The Anschluss* (Philadelphia, 1963); and J. Gehl,
Austria, Germany and the Anschluss, 1931–1938 (London, 1963).
[56] Bullock, *op. cit.*, p. 433. Bullock points out (p. 427) that as
late as March 9, 1938 "the only plan which existed for military action against Austria had been drawn up to prevent Otto of Hapsburg
reclaiming the throne."

HESSE: I have just come back from the Palazzo Venezia.
            The Duce accepted the whole thing in a very
            friendly manner. He sends you his regards. . . .
HITLER: Then please tell Mussolini I will never forget
            him for this.
HESSE: Yes.
HITLER: Never, never, never, whatever happens. . . .
            As soon as the Austrian affair is settled, I shall
            be ready to go with him, through thick and thin,
            no matter what happens.
HESSE: Yes, my Führer.
HITLER: Listen, I shall make any agreement—I am no
            longer in fear of the terrible position which
            would have existed militarily in case we had got
            into a conflict. You may tell him that I thank
            him ever so much; never, never, shall I forget.
HESSE: Yes, my Führer.
HITLER: I will never forget, whatever may happen. If he
            should ever need any help or be in any danger,
            he can be convinced that I shall stick to him,
            whatever may happen, even if the whole world
            were against him.
HESSE: Yes, my Führer.[57]

The fall of Austria to Hitler was second in significance
only to the reoccupation of the Rhineland. Its importance
lay not only in the fact that it gave Germany possession of
a good strategic position from which to attack Czechoslovakia—a factor that was negated to some extent by the
poor road communications between Czechoslovakia and
Austria—but also because it was part of a series of events
between November 1937 and March 1938 that represent a
hardening of Hitler's policies within as well as without the
Nazi state. In November 1937 Hitler announced to his
generals his plans for the absorption of Czechoslovakia;
this was followed in February 1938 by a purge of the Chiefs
of Staff, which marked the end of the coalition of big

[57] Quoted in Bullock, *op. cit.*, p. 431 (Nuremberg, Doc. 2949-PS);
see also p. 438.

business and the military with the Nazi party in favor of complete dominance of the former by the latter.[58] Up to this point Hitler had rejected the necessity or the possibility of war as an instrument of policy; even in Austria, as we have seen, he preferred the method of the gradual internal takeover to the use of open military invasion. But after November 1937, and especially after March 1938, Hitler increasingly contemplated military action, at least against Czechoslovakia. He became more and more convinced that if he was to achieve his ends, Germany would have to fight soon because the British were trying to postpone military conflict at this moment in order to get ready for military conflict in the future. But if Hitler was willing to fight in 1938, he was willing to fight only a particular kind of war, and only because he wished to act before the British grew too strong to threaten him with a war he could not win. Therefore, he preferred to take the risk of war at this time rather than later. For by 1938 the British rearmament program, which had been started in 1935, had begun to take hold; as we have seen, in 1939 Britain's production of aircraft equaled, and her production of tanks excelled, that of Germany. Furthermore, British policy was hardening. Although the Munich conference is always seen as a failure of British diplomacy, and quite rightly so, it also represents a significant turning point in British policy. For the first time since 1919 the British actively, though reluctantly, involved themselves in the affairs of Eastern Europe and demanded that their wishes concerning the area be heard. This was something new, and when it was followed by the British guarantee to Poland and Rumania after Hitler's takeover of all of Czechoslovakia—again in March—in 1939, it was a portent that Hitler would either achieve his aims in Eastern Europe in 1938–1939 or find them increasingly difficult to attain without a major war, a war the issue of which was more and more doubtful from the

[58] See A. Schweitzer, *Big Business in the Third Reich* (Bloomington, Ind., 1964), for a study of the breakup.

German point of view as time went on. This trend, combined with the destruction of whatever restraints big business and the General Staff had exercised on Hitler, meant that, ironically, the years of greatest risk for Hitler lay just ahead. Such a situation was ironical because it occurred when German military power was reaching a peak. Yet, it was just the fact that it was at a peak that caused the element of increased risk. For although German military power was increasing relative to Britain and France in these years, this relative position would soon cease to improve. Even more important, as German military power increased relatively between 1935 and 1939, the willingness of Britain and France to use their power was also increasing. Thus, in 1938–1939, Hitler's chances of achieving his aims without the large-scale, long-term war he wished to avoid were much smaller than in the years 1933–1938 despite the great growth of German military power. It was this increased risk of a major war that Hitler had to face in 1939, when he launched his attack on Poland.[59]

It is therefore irrelevant to ask whether Hitler intended to start World War II, even though there is clear evidence that he did not want such a war and hoped to the end that Britain and France would stay out while he took over Poland.[60] What is decidedly relevant is that Hitler took risks that could and eventually would start a second world war. His increased willingness in November 1937 to take such risks, but also his awareness of and concern over the dangers entailed by those risks, is revealed by the famous Hossbach memorandum of the secret conference between Hitler and his generals, November 5, 1937, during which he explained his plans of operation in the near and distant future. If it was one of Hitler's somewhat theatrical per-

[59] For a brilliant short study of the course of Hitler's policy in these years, see Medlicott's essay, "The Coming of War in 1939," *op. cit.*
[60] See, e.g., *ibid.;* Robertson, *op. cit.,* pp. 181–194; Klein, *op. cit.,* p. 63.

formances, it nevertheless profoundly disturbed the generals who listened to it, and with good reason.

After a long disquisition on the problems of space that faced Germany, Hitler came to the nub of his argument. Given the need for space, "the question for Germany is where the greatest possible conquest could be made at the lowest cost." He then considered the problem.

Germany's problem could only be solved by means of force and this was never without attendant risk. The campaigns of Frederick the Great for Silesia and Bismarck's wars against Austria and France had involved unheard-of risk, and the swiftness of the Prussian action in 1870 had kept Austria from entering the war. If one accepts as the basis of the following exposition the resort to force with its attendant risks, then there remain still to be answered the questions "when" and "how." In this matter there were three cases to be dealt with:

CASE 1: Period 1943–1945.

After this date only a change for the worse, from our point of view, could be expected.

The equipment of the army, navy, and *Luftwaffe,* as well as the formation of the officer corps, was nearly completed. Equipment and armament were modern; in further delay there lay the danger of their obsolescence. In particular, the secrecy of "special weapons" could not be preserved forever. The recruiting of reserves was limited to current age groups; further drafts from older untrained age groups no longer available.

Our relative strength would decrease in relation to the rearmament which would by then have been carried out by the rest of the world. If we did not act by 1943–1945, any year could, in consequence of a lack of reserves, produce the food crisis, to cope with which the necessary foreign exchange was not available, and this must be regarded as a "waning point of the regime." Besides, the world was expecting our attack and was increasing its counter-measures from year to year. It was while the rest of the world was still preparing its defenses that we were obliged to take the offensive.

Nobody knew today what the situation would be in the years 1943-1945. One thing only was certain, that we could not wait longer. On the one hand there was the great *Wehrmacht,* and the necessity of maintaining it at its present level, the aging of the movement and of its leaders; and on the other, the prospect of a lowering of the standard of living and of a limitation of the birth rate, which left no choice but to act. If the Führer was still living, it was his unalterable resolve to solve Germany's problem of space at the latest by 1943-1945. The necessity for action before 1943-1945 would arise in cases 2 and 3.

CASE 2:

If internal strife in France should develop into such a domestic crisis as to absorb the French Army completely and render it incapable of use for war against Germany, then the time for action against the Czechs had come.

CASE 3:

If France is so embroiled by a war with another state that she cannot "proceed" against Germany.

For the improvement of our politico-military position our first objective, in the event of our being embroiled in war, must be to overthrow Czechoslovakia and Austria simultaneously in order to remove the threat to our flank in any possible operation against the West. In a conflict with France it was hardly to be regarded as likely that the Czechs would declare war on us on the very same day as France. The desire to join in the war would, however, increase among the Czechs in proportion to any weakening on our part and then her participation could clearly take the form of an attack toward Silesia, toward the north or toward the west.

If the Czechs were overthrown and a common German-Hungarian frontier achieved, a neutral attitude on the part of Poland could be the more certainly counted on in the event of a Franco-German conflict. Our agreements with Poland only retained their force as long as Germany's strength remained unshaken. In the event of German setbacks a Polish action against East Prussia, and possibly against Pomerania and Silesia as well, had to be reckoned with.

On the assumption of a development of the situation leading to action on our part as planned, in the years 1943–1945, the attitude of France, Britain, Italy, Poland, and Russia could probably be estimated as follows:

Actually, the Führer believed that almost certainly Britain, and probably France as well, had already tacitly written off the Czechs and were reconciled to the fact that this question would be cleared up in due course by Germany. Difficulties connected with the Empire, and the prospect of being once more entangled in a protracted European war, were decisive considerations for Britain against participation in a war against Germany. Britain's attitude would certainly not be without influence on that of France. An attack by France without British support, and with the prospect of the offensive being brought to a standstill on our western fortifications, was hardly probable. Nor was a French march through Belgium and Holland without British support to be expected; this also was a course not to be contemplated by us in the event of a conflict with France, because it would certainly entail the hostility of Britain. It would of course be necessary to maintain a strong defense on our western frontier during the prosecution of our attack on the Czechs and Austria. And in this connection it had to be remembered that the defense measures of the Czechs were growing in strength from year to year, and that the actual worth of the Austrian Army also was increasing in the course of time. Even though the populations concerned, especially of Czechoslovakia, were not sparse, the annexation of Czechoslovakia and Austria would mean an acquisition of foodstuffs for 5 to 6 million people, on the assumption that the compulsory emigration of 2 million people from Czechoslovakia and 1 million people from Austria was practicable. The incorporation of these two States with Germany meant, from the politico-military point of view, a substantial advantage because it would mean shorter and better frontiers, the freeing of forces for other purposes, and the possibility of creating new units up to a level of about 12 divisions, that is 1 new division per million inhabitants.

Italy was not expected to object to the elimination of the Czechs, but it was impossible at the moment to estimate what her attitude on the Austrian question would be; that depended essentially upon whether the Duce were still alive.

The degree of surprise and the swiftness of our action were decisive factors for Poland's attitude. Poland—with Russia at her rear—will have little inclination to engage in war against a victorious Germany.

Military intervention by Russia must be countered by the swiftness of our operations; however, whether such an intervention was a practical contingency at all was, in view of Japan's attitude, more than doubtful.

Should case 2 arise—the crippling of France by civil war— the situation thus created by the elimination of the most dangerous opponent must be seized upon *whenever it occurs* for the blow against the Czechs.

The Führer saw case 3 coming definitely nearer; it might emerge from the present tensions in the Mediterranean, and he was resolved to take advantage of it whenever it happened, even as early as 1938.[61]

The reactions of General von Blomberg, Reichminister for War, and General von Fritsch, Commander-in-Chief of the Army, to this rather confused analysis are not without significance.

In appraising the situation Field Marshal von Blomberg and Colonel General von Fritsch repeatedly emphasized the necessity that Britain and France must not appear in the role of our enemies, and stated that the French Army would not be so committed by the war with Italy that France

---

[61] DGFP, Ser. D, Vol. I, Doc. 19. Italics in original.

could not at the same time enter the field with forces superior to ours on our western frontier. General von Fritsch estimated the probable French forces available for use on the Alpine frontier at approximately twenty divisions, so that a strong French superiority would still remain on the western frontier, with the role, according to the German view, of invading the Rhineland. In this matter, moreover, the advanced state of French defense preparations must be taken into particular account, and it must be remembered apart from the insignificant value of our present fortification—on which Field Marshal von Blomberg laid special emphasis—that the four motorized divisions intended for the West were still more or less incapable of movement. In regard to our offensive toward the southeast, Field Marshal von Blomberg drew particular attention to the strength of the Czech fortifications, which had acquired by now a structure like a Maginot Line and which would gravely hamper our attack.[62]

The Führer tried to soothe his agitated generals by repeating that "he was convinced of Britain's nonparticipation and that consequently he did not believe in military action by France against Germany." [63]

There are several points of interest about this conference, which throw considerable light on Hitler's objectives and the risks he was willing to take to achieve them. First, it will be noticed that, as A. J. P. Taylor has pointed out, if Hitler's talk is to be taken as a plan of action, it was not a very accurate plan since his speculations bear little relationship to what actually happened.[64] Second, it is obvious that Hitler was far from contemplating a general war at this time

[62] *Ibid.*
[63] *Ibid.*
[64] A. J. P. Taylor, *The Origins of the Second World War* (New York, 1962), p. 134. This stimulating and intriguing work has many useful insights and the great virtue of reexamining the evidence from a point of view completely at variance with the standard interpretations of this period. Yet some of its conclusions are misleading, and therefore it must be used with great caution. For a balanced view of this work, see F. H. Hinsley, *Power and the Pursuit of Peace* (Cambridge, England, 1963), Ch. 15.

and preferably not at any time. Third, the document indicates that Hitler recognized that internal politics, particularly in France, as well as international politics as it affected France and, even more importantly, Britain would be crucial to his plans. Fourth, Hitler was able to contemplate military action in Eastern Europe only on the premise that Britain and France would not act against him. Fifth, and most important, the document reveals that whatever the inadequacy and even naiveté of his plans and expectations in respect to other states, Hitler was contemplating actions that would put him in a position where general war would be a possible outcome. It was his willingness to take this risk, and not just the specifics of his ideas, that must have horrified the generals who listened to him. It was this willingness to take this gamble that finally brought about World War II.

Yet, despite this risktaking, the exertion of political and military pressure on Hitler by Britain and France up through the *Anschluss* and especially in the reoccupation of the Rhineland would almost certainly have led to Hitler's political defeat in the international arena. It is also significant that Hitler did not use the threat of war as a means of gaining his objectives until the Munich crisis of 1938. But pressures were not brought to bear on him, and because the balance of military power was increasingly closer to an equilibrium, Hitler was in a position in 1938–1939 to attempt an even greater risk than those he had so successfully tried earlier, despite the fact that there was less chance of success this time due to the increased involvement of Britain in continental Europe. He knew that his chances of success were growing smaller—which is why he hurried forward. The balance of power was beginning to operate and to once again create a potential preponderance of power on the side of Britain and France, but there was a brief moment before the readjustment of the balance had been completed when there was a chance for him to take his greatest risk and possibly get away with it.

Hitler's Diplomatic Methods and the Balance of Power

Discussions of the events of the 1930's must not only focus on the failure of Britain and France to take effective action in the face of Hitler's maneuvers but also on the particular quality of his diplomatic methods. It was these methods that created the new situation in which the balance of power had to function if it was to function at all. Because Hitler's diplomatic methods as well as his intentions—the two cannot be divorced from one another—produced that situation, it is imperative to understand their essential nature so that the special essence of this *type* of diplomatic situation can be grasped. Only then will it be possible to isolate and study the unique problems it created for the operation of the balance of power.

It was a type of situation that presented few if any of the features of the classical power balances and few of the prerequisites that are so often laid down for an effective balance of power by theorists of international relations. But because this set of conditions does not fit the classical model there is no reason to assume that the balance could not have been used successfully as a means of achieving stability. Rather than making that assumption, it is better to look upon this period not as one in which the balance is inoperable because it violates the abstract rules laid down by theory but as one that poses problems for the use of the balance. As we have seen, there is good reason to think that the balance could have restrained Hitler. And as we shall see, it was the failure of Chamberlain to understand the special qualities of the new type of situation created by Hitler's diplomatic methods that brought about the failure of his policies.

Two aspects of Hitler's diplomatic methods created this new type of diplomatic situation, and hence identify its essential characteristics.

1. Throughout this period Hitler played what might be called a pseudobroker role. He played it intermittently, but with a shrewd sense of timing. Whatever Hitler's intentions may have been about starting a second world war, at no time was he willing to assume the role of a broker, to perform as a leader between his own state and the leaders of other states in presenting and accepting demands. But he did play *at* the part, imitating the role without ever acting out its substance. Hitler came into an international system based on brokerage both as a way of keeping the system going *and* as a way of changing it in certain important respects (as was done, for example, at Locarno). His rejection of this method for both purposes was total and complete. It is ironical that a clever use of the brokerage role, as Stresemann might have used it, would have gained for Germany many of Hitler's basic aims and have put her into a position of dominance within continental Europe, since Britain was ready at this time to make far-reaching concessions to Germany and to liquidate the Versailles system once and for all. But such a position of dominance would have still had to take place within the framework of a balance of power. It is because he rejected that framework as such that Hitler could not and would not play the brokerage role.[65] But the pseudo-use of the role was important to him since it enabled him to divide his enemies—as in the German-Polish nonaggression treaty and the Anglo-German Naval Agreement—and also to pretend that he would consider the demands of other states as well as present his own demands to them. This pretense, the distinguishing trait of pseudobrokerage, made it possible for him to take actions that undermined the balance of power while he presented himself to the outside world as a leader who only sought to modify the balance. The rule of Hitler's diplomacy was

[65] Obviously there were other reasons. One was probably his own personality, while another was the fact that totalitarian regimes, because of their very nature and their ideology, find it difficult—though not necessarily impossible—to play this essentially bourgeois role.

this: For every act that helped destroy the balance of power system, an offer should be made to bring brokerage into operation for the purpose of maintaining the system. We have seen how Hitler did this in both the crisis of 1935 and the Rhineland crisis of 1936, and he maintained his rule until very late in the period; even after the Munich crisis he solemnly went through a process of signing an agreement with Britain to the effect that the two states would cooperate and consult with each other on their further demands, the famous piece of paper that Chamberlain waved to the crowd upon his arrival back in London and that he said assured peace in our time. Until Munich, pseudobrokerage was important to Hitler as a cover for his own military weakness because it enabled him to present his moves as simply an attempt to readjust the balance. He was able to do so because up to March 1939 his acts *could* have been seen in these terms *if* he was in fact willing to play the role of a broker. It was exactly this possibility that Hitler used to convince Britain and France—but especially Britain—that *they* should play the broker's role. The significance of Hitler's use of the pseudobrokerage role was that it caused a radical dichotomy, not only in the relationships between Britain and France on the one hand and Germany on the other, but within the structure of the balance of power system itself.

2. The complement to this playing *at* the broker's role on the part of Hitler was his risktaking. Obviously, the acts of all states, and all human activity, for that matter, involve risk to a greater or lesser degree. What is referred to here, however, is a form of diplomatic activity that will not use or accept brokerage, tacit or explicit, as a means of achieving the foreign policy aims of a state and that rejects the whole basis and concept of brokerage. As a result, the diplomacy of such a state is based on a totally different idea of what international relations is about than the ideas held by those who use brokerage. The risktaker is at the

opposite pole from the broker. He sees international relations as incapable of producing a bargain or gain of any kind unless it is achieved by the defeat, as total as possible, of other states. Hence, he can only achieve his aims by taking risks, for the only way a state can get something from another state is by an action that *inherently* holds the risk that other states will strike back because the risktaker is getting something without simultaneously accepting the idea of limits to his activity. It is an either/or world that this type of state inhabits because either the risktaking state is defeated or the other states are defeated. Because this is so, the risktaker must take the risks that result from acting without consent, since, in his view, other states would not grant him what he wants under any other circumstances.

He is correct in thinking so, because essentially what such a state wants is the absence of restraint on her actions; the risktaker's aim of destroying restraint and his use of risktaking as a method of diplomacy are indissolubly intertwined. The risktaker is a state whose concept of international relations makes it necessary for her to reject any demands made upon her, even if they would lead to part of what she wants, through a system of brokerage, as they did in the diplomacy of Stresemann. Hence the risktaker rejects the idea of restraint on the part of the members of an international system and the whole idea of the balance of power. He is outside the law of the balance of power and, as an outlaw, actively works to destroy the balance of power *as a system* and not simply a particular balance of power. He rejects the very idea of the balance—of any balance—as restraint because he is as totalitarian in foreign policy as in domestic politics, seeing *only* victory or defeat in politics, international or otherwise. The broker sees partial victories, partial defeats, and the advantages of the restraint that partial victory and defeat bring with them. The risktaker is totalitarian because outside of total victory there is nothing. Since he acknowledges no restraint from the outside, he must actively work against the very idea itself as it is embodied in the system of balance.

In summary, the risktaker in international relations may be conceptualized as a state whose diplomatic methods create the risk that other states will strike back with force, military or other, because brokerage is rejected. Such a state will reject brokerage even if it is offered because she is actively attacking the concept of restraint in the sphere of international relations. She is the counterpart in international relations to the totalitarian state in the domestic life of a nation, since both reject all restraint and both seek total power. (It should be added that the two forms of totalitarianism do not necessarily go together, though, in fact, the one will probably be found with the other.)

Obviously, the risktaker is conceived and described here as a polar type at one end of a continuum, at the opposite end of which lies the broker. Hence, in fact, all states in real life partake of some aspects of both activities to a greater or lesser degree. Hitler Germany, however, was as close to the pure concept of risktaking as any actual state is likely to be. Hitler took precisely those actions that the balance of power was designed to prevent and that, therefore, threatened to bring it into operation against him. He was wary about attacking the Locarno balance directly. But he deliberately refused to work within the restrictions set by the idea of a balance itself. As a result, every action he took, no matter how shrewd or even reasonable it may have seemed or been made to seem, necessarily involved the gigantic risk of bringing the balance of power into operation in order to save the principle of the balance itself. In every case this was the issue that Hitler's acts raised: Should the balance of power be used against him? It was not only the specifics, the provisions of Locarno, which were at stake in the 1930's. Far more important was the very principle of Locarno itself. Hitler knew this. So did those who were opposed to him. But he was forced into these risks, not only because of the difficulty of obtaining his objectives through a system of brokerage, but because of his repudiation of the whole idea of the balance. One can be relatively certain that other German leaders in the 1930's, say another Stresemann or a German general such as von Schleicher, would have sought many of the objectives sought by Hitler. They, too, would have made the effort to reestablish a German armed force, to reoccupy the Rhine, to carry out the *Anschluss*. But, it is equally certain that they would not have taken the risks that Hitler took and that they would, therefore, have sought their objects through a system of brokerage and within the system of a new balance of power. Such a balance would have been similar to that envisaged by Austen Chamberlain during the Locarno negotiations, in which German power in Eastern Europe would have been balanced by the safeguard of French independence in the West through Britain's "watch on the Rhine." It is almost certain that such German leaders would not have threatened France directly, just as it is certain that French influence on the continent would have shrunk. Something approaching the pre-1914 situation would have reemerged, with German power in Eastern Europe playing the role of the Austrian-Hungarian Empire through its political and economic influence, but without overt military conquest. Thus, although Germany would have gained much of what she wanted, limits on her power would have been established through a system of brokerage, tacit or overt, as the case might have been.

Hitler did not follow this path. He rejected it not only because of his specific foreign policy aims; as we have just seen, many of those could have been more securely achieved by other methods and within the framework of a balance of power. (It is worth pointing out that if those other methods had been used, Germany would today be the greatest power in Europe and a world power rather than being divided into two states.)

Hitler's diplomatic methods did not partake only of the qualitative aspects of risktaking described above. His methods also had a quantitative aspect in the sense that he took more and greater risks than did other leaders of that time or, perhaps, of any time in modern international relations, the activities of Napoleon notwithstanding. Hitler, therefore, presents an instance of an extreme form of behavior in which other leaders also engage. The fact of this extremism is important, for by its very nature it posed a serious problem to other leaders. Because his behavior was so far from the norm, from the midrange of risktaking, it was difficult to identify, difficult to believe that he was actually taking such risks. Hence, the propensity of the leaders of Britain and France to overestimate the strength of Germany and their difficulty in even knowing when Hitler was taking a risk. But even if the extreme degree of risktaking in which he indulged had been recognized for what it was, there remained the problem of how to deal with it. Again, precisely because Hitler's actions in this realm of behavior were so far outside the norm, there was little experience on which to draw in meeting this particular kind of threat. The experience was gained over the decade of the 1930's, but too late to make the balance operate effectively in the light of that experience. How to meet this degree of risktaking was one of the crucial questions Hitler presented to the chancelleries of Europe. Not only was the answer not as obvious then as it is often assumed to be today, but the very question posed a profoundly difficult dilemma, as we shall see below in a consideration of Chamberlain's foreign policy.

The risktaker, who has been described here as a totalitarian outlaw who rejects the fundamental postulates of restraint and constraint in a balance of power system and the system of brokerage on which it is based, is a polar abstract type at the opposite end of a continuum from the broker. Hitler and Stresemann, both from the same nation and in the same period of history, may be said to represent these two types. The situation that is created by the diplomatic methods of a risktaker, a Hitler, is also a type of situation that is characterized by the problem of how to coerce the risktaker into the role of a broker. For if this coercion is not achieved, the risktaker may bring about a major war, either on purpose or inadvertently through his risktaking, which will mean the end of the balance of power as a system of restraint.[66] It does not follow that because the risktaker has the characteristics described above he cannot be made to accept brokerage. But, obviously, to do so, coercive power will have to be used. Hitler's willingness to take risks of the nature and magnitude that other German leaders would not have taken sets the problem that the risktaker poses to the defenders of the balance as a system.

But to say that the risktaker can be coerced into broker-age is, however, only to make a general statement from a safe distance and well away from the responsibilities of power. Manifestly, this type of balance of power situation creates extremely complex problems of choice of means and timing. How, in fact, could the defenders of the balance coerce the risktaker into brokerage? It also requires a sensi-tive awareness to the fact that this type of balance of power situation has arisen. The difficulties and dilemmas of oper-ating a balance of power in this type of situation can be seen by a consideration of British and French diplomacy after 1933.

The British and French Response to Hitler

The type of situation created by Hitler's diplomatic methods posed a particular set of problems for the operation of the balance of power. It has just been stated that those states whose aim it was to maintain the balance in the 1930's could have demonstrated the weaknesses of Hitler's position and forced him to acknowledge his limitations at least

[66] The degree to which Hitler's actions had their origins in his personality and especially in suicide-proneness has been interestingly examined by J. H. McRandle, *The Track of the Wolf: Essays on National Socialism and Its Leader, Adolf Hitler* (Evanston, Ill., 1965), Ch. 5.

before 1938. But the question was and is in this type of situation: How could this be done without the overt conflict and war that might easily destroy the balance in the process by triggering off a general conflict? How could Hitler's activities be limited without starting a second world war that would bring the balance of power to an end and mean its failure as a method of restraint? Risktaking of the type in which Hitler engaged and the rejection of brokerage on the part of one member of the balance open up the possibility and dilemma that the only way to preserve the balance is to take the immense risk of starting a war of such scale that the balance itself would be demolished. It, therefore, forces the defenders of the balance to consider another alternative. This is to discover ways that would make the risktaker adopt the role of a broker. For only if the risktaker can be converted to such a role can limits be set to his activities and to the power of his state without the dangerous use of overt conflict and war. At the very least, this alternative will minimize the chances that war would break out in the process of preserving the balance. Such a policy would, therefore, preserve the balance with a minimum of conflict and hence with a maximum of efficiency. It is a policy that is clearly superior to meeting the risktaker with overt conflict—if it works. Which is not to say that it cannot be made to work. It is, however, to say that it requires the most scrupulous timing and the most precise use of power to make it a successful policy. It was with the difficulties created by those requirements that Chamberlain and those who went before him in the conduct of British foreign policy had to deal.

Chamberlain tried to execute this alternative through a policy of appeasement, which was a policy designed to make Hitler accept the role of a broker. The *effectiveness* with which this policy was pursued will be evaluated below, but here it must be emphasized that, as a policy, appeasement is not an act of weakness. In this case, it cannot be viewed only as an act of weakness in which Britain and France

gave way to Germany's power, for the origins of this instance of appeasement lay in the period when Britain and
France possessed more military power than Germany—
which is not to say that the same policy did not become an
act of weakness when it was continued in other circumstances, namely in 1938. Rather, it was an attempt to come
to some sort of agreement with Hitler on various issues and
by the very act of making an agreement deflect him from
risktaking, from challenging the balance of power to come
into operation against him and force him into brokerage,
that is, into working with the other members of the balance
as a broker in the full sense of the concept as defined
earlier. The magnitude and importance of this endeavor
must be recognized, for the difficulties of this task demonstrate the problems posed by a risktaker to the defenders
of a balance. For such an endeavor to be successful Hitler
must assume and accept the fundamental qualities of brokerage; he must act in the mode of a Stresemann. Hence,
he must carry demands back and forth between his own
political system and that of the balance and must not only
seek to represent and attain the interests of the former but
also manipulate his political system in the interests of the
balance of power. He must not simply put forth demands
but work with the members of the balance to satisfy their
demands. Hitler would have to divorce himself to a degree
from his own political system in order to tell it what it
could not, as well as what it could, achieve. Since it was
obvious that Hitler was no Stresemann, the problem that
this endeavor posed was to what extent Hitler could be
made to conform to the broker's model and what means
could bring about his acceptance of this role.

Chamberlain believed that achieving this objective was
more important than any one question at issue between
Britain and Germany; he believed that the crucial need
of British and French foreign policy was not to preserve
the political map rigidly unchanged but to preserve the
essential features of the balance of power. In order to do

so it was necessary to bring Hitler into the balance and to get him to accept demands, that is, limits on his acts, as well as to make demands. Chamberlain, and Eden before him, recognized early that they were dealing with an extraordinary individual, to say the least, and while there was a large element of self-delusion and overweening egoism in Chamberlain's personality and in his approach to this problem, there was also a recognition on his part that it was only through the conversion of Hitler from a risktaker to a broker that the balance could be preserved without a world war. For if this conversion could not be accomplished, the alternative, as Chamberlain saw it, was the collapse of the whole principle of the balance of power, either through a slow erosion or through overt and general war. Appeasement was to be the means of maintaining the basic principle of the balance of power.

It was to be *the* balance of power, however, that was to be preserved, not *a* balance of power. To convert Hitler from a risktaker to a broker would necessarily involve an attempt on the part of Chamberlain and those who preceded him in the control of British foreign policy to change or modify the then current balance of power, essentially that of 1925, in order to meet some of the German demands—in order, that is, to increase German power within the framework of the restraints and limits that are an essential feature of a balance. Chamberlain's policy was not, most emphatically not, to prevent change in the balance. Quite the contrary, his policy, the whole idea of appeasement, was to modify or change the balance in such a way that Hitler would find it profitable to accept the role of a broker because he could achieve some—some, not all—of his aims through that procedure and hence afford to accept demands from other states.

Any attempt to change a given balance or to replace it with a new and different one is bound to be a complex process extending over a considerable length of time under the best of circumstances since a balance has inertia and

the status quo built into it. Furthermore, once the issue
of changing a balance is raised, the already established
balance is put into doubt; instability is created by the very
act of raising the question of change, a fact of which Hitler
took full advantage. Such instability may be very difficult
to control in what may be called the transitional period
and may wreck the whole procedure since the restraints of
the balance are weakened by that instability. Yet the attempt must be made if there is to be any hope of order in
international relations, since balances cannot endure forever, and change is necessary. Orderly change through a
process of brokerage is more desirable than striking a new
balance after conflict. It was the accomplishment of this
difficult task that Chamberlain attempted by his policy of
appeasement—and under the most unfavorable circumstances.

But the process of changing a balance poses an even more
acute problem than that of the inherent instability of the
transition period. *Can* the balance be changed? Is there
any real alternative to the current distribution of power
that will be acceptable to those participating in the balance
and at the same time provide for a system of restraint?
Given a particular configuration of the political map, with
the drives and ambitions of the states that make it up, is
only one distribution of power possible for a system of
restraint and balance? Even assuming a process of brokerage, and thus a willingness to work within the framework
of the balance on the part of the state demanding change,
the question would arise of whether or not it is possible
to conceive of a different distribution of power that would
maintain a balance between the same states who were a
party to the old balance. Chamberlain had to face this
general problem in terms of concrete questions. During the
1930's, what other distribution of power than that of 1925
was possible as a system of restraints? Should Germany
be allowed to expand into Eastern Europe, for instance?
If so, how far? In what form? With what safeguards?

Could such expansion be checked and limited to certain predetermined boundaries? What would such expansion mean for the power of the states of Western Europe, and especially for France? Would it require a counterincrease in British and French power, in order to balance off the increase that would accrue to Germany in Eastern Europe, and also a tightening of the relationship between Britain and France? If so, would not the whole exercise lead to the creation of more armaments and a system of alliances that would increase tension within Europe? Were the British and French publics willing to pay this price for satisfying German demands in Eastern Europe?

These questions indicate the complexity of the process of changing a balance as a general proposition. In particular, they are the problems that Chamberlain would have had to face and resolve under the best of circumstances, that is, if there had been a government in Germany that would have been ready to act the role of a broker.

But manifestly, circumstances were not of the best. In order to resolve these difficult and complex problems Hitler had to be converted to brokerage so that a new system of balance could be established. Appeasement as a concept of how this conversion should be attempted was, as far as it went, a sound and logical effort to get the system of brokerage into operation through a process of mutual concession. If Chamberlain carried Hitler's demands back to the British political system, Hitler too had to appease the British, so to speak, by carrying their demands back to his political system. Once that process was started, risktaking would be minimized, and thus, too, the possibility that the coercive power of the balance would be brought into play. To put it more concisely, the possibility of war would be minimized.

The failure of this policy in the 1930's resulted from the inability or refusal of Britain's leaders to understand that modification or change in the balance through appeasement required not only concessions by Britain but also that de-

gree of coercion that would force Hitler to adopt a policy
of brokerage. Because the British did not see the need for
coercion until very late in the 1930's, they timed their
moves in such a way that they could not achieve their objective of converting Hitler to brokerage. In the type of
diplomatic situation created by a risktaker such as Hitler,
appeasement without coercion will give him the opportunity to do what he aims to do, that is, to destroy the system of restraint embodied in a balance of power by refusing the role of a broker. He will do so even if he is in
a position of military inferiority since, as we have seen,
it is precisely his objective to destroy the principle of the
balance itself. Obviously, appeasement without coercion
applied to a risktaker such as Hitler when a position of
military equilibrium exists enables the risktaker to depend
on a technical breakthrough or simply on risk itself and
thus to ignore any offers that are made to him. However,
and most important, even if appeasement is backed by
coercion in a situation of military equilibrium, the risktaker will depend on technical breakthrough as a means of
destroying the balance. But if coercion is used with appeasement in order to convert a risktaker to brokerage in
a situation in which the risktaker is in a position of military
inferiority, he has no alternative but to accept the role of
a broker. For he cannot depend on technical breakthrough
or on risk either because he has no chance of succeeding in
his risk or because his chances are minimal. As we have
seen, Hitler was aware of these various alternatives and
operated accordingly. The British were not, and, hence,
they timed their acts in precisely the opposite way from
which they should have if they were to achieve their aim
of converting Hitler to brokerage. In the period 1933-
1938 they tried appeasement without coercion. It was in
that period that appeasement supported by coercion might
well have succeeded. But in 1938, during the height of
the Munich crisis, they suddenly attempted coercion in
conjunction with appeasement after Chamberlain's second

conference with Hitler at Godesberg—and they backed down from it. They backed down because by that time it was too late to try a policy of coercion with appeasement, since a military equilibrium at the very least had been achieved by Hitler. It should be added that the refusal of appeasement by a preponderant power or group of powers can also create a complex set of problems. Preponderance of power without appeasement can frighten even the most well-intentioned state and in some situations cause it to take actions designed to undermine or weaken the power of the dominant state, hence creating tension and conflict. But where a risktaker is involved, the situation is even more complicated. For a preponderant power to *refuse* appeasement to a risktaker is to foreclose the possibility that its preponderance can be used to convert a risktaker to brokerage. These are the difficulties of choice for a preponderant status quo power that are created by a risktaker. Preponderance of power in the real world is not something total in its effect or that can ignore the needs and interests of other states.

Appeasement was a legitimate search for a way to resolve the problem created by Hitler's foreign policy without resorting to the general war, which in and of itself would mean the failure of the balance of power. But it can only convert a risktaker such as Hitler to brokerage under the one circumstance defined above. For it is the essence of the type of diplomatic situation created by this kind of risktaker that he brutally and consciously destroys alternative policies.

Between 1933 and 1938 Britain treated Hitler as if he were a broker, another Stresemann, who could be brought into the system of brokerage because he accepted the balance of power as such and would thus accept another Locarno. By the fall of 1938, during the height of the Sudeten crisis, Britain suddenly shifted to a weak attempt to coerce Hitler into accepting the role of a broker. This lag in the adjustment to a new balance of power situation

—mainly the responsibility of Britain—raises the question of why the lag took place. The answer may throw some light on the vital and more general question of the ability of the balance of power system to meet new situations and especially on whether or not the system itself is the source of some of the difficulties of adjusting a balance of power system to new political forces. A consideration of Anglo-French diplomacy after 1933 will make it possible to offer an answer to these problems.

It was at Munich that British efforts to convert Hitler to brokerage came to a climax and where their difficulties were most vividly demonstrated. But by the time the Munich conference took place, it was almost certainly too late for this effort to succeed. The notoriety of the Munich conference has obscured the fact and significance of the efforts that preceded it. For it was these efforts that could have been successful if they had been properly used; at Munich it is doubtful if appeasement in any form could have been successful. A study of appeasement must go back to its sources in the very first days of Hitler's regime and the earliest series of moves on the part of Britain and France to deal with the problem presented by Hitler.

The first Anglo-French essay in appeasement after Hitler's rise to power was the Four Power Pact of July 1933.[67] The significance of this agreement lies not in what it accomplished, which was virtually nothing at all, but in the way it symbolizes the British ideal of how the affairs of Europe should be organized, namely, through a four-power condominium composed of Britain, France, Italy, and Germany. The Great Powers were to work together because a process of brokerage would be established that would make it possible for each power to obtain the agreement of the other powers on how it was to manipulate the smaller states of Europe. Or, to put it in plain language,

[67] Furnia, *op. cit.*, p. 80, claims that the proposal originated with Britain and not Mussolini as is usually assumed.

four-power brokerage would define the spheres of influence of each power. So naked was this suggestion in the original pact that France insisted, in deference to her allies in Eastern Europe, that it be disguised and watered down. Thus, the final draft simply read that "the High Contracting Parties will consult together as regards all questions which appertain to them," and that "they undertake to make every effort to pursue, within the framework of the League of Nations, a policy of effective cooperation between all Powers with a view to the maintenance of Peace" (Art. 1). They also agreed that they would decide how the decisions of the League would be implemented (Art. 2). The meaning of these innocent phrases was not lost on anyone, least of all the states of Eastern Europe; Poland even went to the extent of temporarily seeking the friendship of the Soviet Union in the face of this threat of four-power domination and Franco-German collaboration.[68] The states of Eastern Europe were saved from this threat, however, not only by the French refusal to take the pact seriously, but also by Hitler's rejection of this offer of a system of brokerage when he left the League of Nations in October 1933. The French were fearful that Germany would use this pact to further her plans for revisionism, and Hitler feared that the British would use the pact to tie down and restrict his plans for expansion. Both were correct. The real implications of the pact can be seen in the original proposals that France rejected and that recognized the need for specific territorial changes in Eastern Europe; for example, the establishment of a territorial connection between East Prussia and Germany and the return of Danzig to Germany.[69] The pact, therefore, demonstrates clearly, at the very beginning of the Hitler epoch, what has

[68] B. B. Budurowycz, *Polish-Soviet Relations, 1932–1939* (New York, 1963), p. 30; see G. A. Craig and F. Gilbert, eds., *The Diplomats, 1919–1939* (paperback ed., New York, 1963), Vol. I, p. 120.
[69] Furnia, *op. cit.*, pp. 81–84.

been called the four-power policy of Britain,[70] a policy
that was at the heart of appeasement. It is no coincidence
that it was the same four powers that met together at
Munich in 1938 to offer Germany a decisive control of
Eastern Europe—or, perhaps more accurately, to recognize
her decisive control of Eastern Europe. The outlines of
Munich were clearly foreshadowed in the Four Power Pact
of 1933.

It was because the four-power policy ran counter to
French plans to use the states of Eastern Europe as a
"barrier" that France, under the leadership of Barthou
(foreign minister from February to October 1934), di-
verged from British policy and attempted to strike out on
her own in an attempt to form a coalition against Germany.
In 1935 the most striking success of this policy was the
signing of the Franco-Soviet treaty of mutual assistance
despite the opposition of the British. Discussions on this
treaty were accompanied by a French plan for an Eastern
Locarno, a system of pacts that would have brought the
Soviet Union squarely into Eastern Europe as a guarantor
of the status quo in that area and even into Western
Europe by making her a guarantor of the borders of France,
and thus a part of the Locarno Pact of 1925.[71] Manifestly,
such a system was designed to prevent any expansion of
Germany in the East, while bringing the Soviet Union into
an anti-German coalition. Needless to say, the Germans
refused to have anything to do with such an arrangement,
although for tactical reasons they found it advisable to
treat the plan with respect. But the British were angry at

[70] E. R. Cameron, *Prologue to Appeasement: A Study in French
Foreign Policy* (Washington, D.C., 1942), pp. 28-36, 197-199, 201-
206.
[71] The Eastern Locarno arrangement was to be a treaty of mutual
aid signed by the Soviet Union, Germany, Poland, Czechoslovakia,
Lithuania, Latvia, Estonia, and Finland. France would guarantee the
pact through a separate treaty signed with the Soviet Union; the
latter in turn would guarantee the Locarno Pact of 1925 and thus
pledge herself to come to the aid of France.

the whole idea. Sir John Simon, then foreign secretary of Britain, saw it as an encircling alliance of the prewar type and said privately that "if France continues along that line England may make a deal with Germany and Belgium. . . ." [72] The British became more favorably inclined when the French agreed to their suggestion that France should give Germany a guarantee against Russia and Russia give Germany a guarantee against France—an idea that Barthou treated with the cynicism it deserved. Barthou was also forced to agree that France would consider negotiations for an arms convention giving Germany equality of arms.[73] But not only the Germans and British were hostile to the Eastern Locarno idea. The Poles also refused to enter such a pact, since the last thing they wanted was the Soviet Union coming to the aid of Poland.

The stimulus to the Franco-Soviet treaty came from Hitler's announcement of the rearmament of Germany in defiance of the Versailles Treaty. Once again, however, the British reaction differed from that of the French. The British foreign secretary, instead of forming an alliance against Hitler, took a trip to Berlin for conversations, the object of which was to find out whether or not Hitler would agree to join a system of mutual security in the West, which the British and French (under British prodding and in a period of temporary disenchantment with the Soviet Union) had proposed in February 1935. These were proposals for a "general settlement freely negotiated between Germany and the other Powers." Specifically, they had suggested the Eastern Locarno arrangement, Danubian pacts of a similar type, equality of rights in armaments for Germany through negotiation, German membership in the League of Nations, and an air pact that would provide for aid by the forces of Germany, Italy, Belgium, Britain, and France to

[72] Quoted in Scott, *op. cit.*, p. 172. For a useful summary of the Eastern Locarno proposal, see Scott, pp. 166–177.
[73] *Ibid.*, pp. 179–180.

any member of the pact who was the victim of unprovoked air attack. The latter pact was carefully limited to Western Europe, and hence would have had the effect of weakening French ties with their allies in Eastern Europe. It was these schemes that the British foreign secretary wished to discuss with Hitler, even after the latter had announced the unilateral rearmament of Germany. The refusal of Hitler to consider any of these schemes, with the possible exception of the air pact—on which, however, the British put great store—was a rude shock to Britain. The conclusions drawn by the British were that Germany still wanted good relations with Britain but that Germany had no intention of joining a system of collective security. The latter conclusion, at least, was correct.

At this particular instance—early 1935—Anglo-French cooperation was momentarily flourishing at the very time that Franco-Russian collaboration was in the making. An effective encirclement of Hitler was now a definite possibility. But this possibility of a revived triple entente vanished under the divisive impact of the Ethiopian War, the Spanish Civil War, the refusal of the French Government to implement the Franco-Soviet Pact, and the Anglo-German Naval Agreement.

The Ethiopian War posed Anglo-French relations with an acute dilemma, since the French had been pursuing a policy of friendship with Mussolini in order to win him over to a policy of encircling Germany. This policy had achieved the first sign of success when Mussolini had stopped the Nazi attempt to take over Austria in 1934, and a second sign of success in Laval's trip to Rome in January 1935, when the Franco-Italian agreements were signed. In these agreements both states consented to support the independence of Austria, and Laval, in private conversation, at least implicitly agreed to Mussolini's penetration and eventual domination of Ethiopia. But when Mussolini openly invaded Ethiopia the French and the British found themselves divided on whom to appease. The

French wanted to appease Italy in order to maintain the encirclement of Germany; the British wanted to appease Germany in order to be free to block Italian expansion in the Mediterranean and to maintain the principles of the League of Nations for which they showed a sudden attachment in view of Mussolini's aggression. The Hoare-Laval plan was an attempt to reconcile these demands, but in essence it gave Mussolini what he wanted. Unfortunately, the outcry of the British public caused Baldwin to seek the easy way out, which was to dismiss Sir Samuel Hoare as foreign secretary and to follow a policy of sanctions, which, by this time (December 1935), was too late to be effective. The worst of all possible worlds was the net result of this crisis for the West. Mussolini got Ethiopia and wrecked the League in the process; yet he was alienated from Britain and France and thrust into the waiting arms of Hitler. It was the latter who also gained the most from the Spanish Civil War, for in Spain, Britain and France were once again entangled with Italy in the Mediterranean area, with the additional complication that Soviet aid to the Spanish Republic raised the fear of a Communist state on the border of France among the leaders of Britain and France. Soviet policy in Spain finished any chance that the Franco-Soviet treaty might have had of becoming an effective block to Hitler. However, it had never had any real chance of becoming effective, since French governments had never followed up the pact with a military convention and had never taken steps to implement it.[74]

Instead, the French moved closer to Britain once the Ethiopian War had been liquidated. As we have seen, when the Rhine crisis broke in March 1936, the French either could not or would not move without the support of Britain. It is from this point that France irrevocably subordinated her diplomacy to that of Britain and to all intents and purposes gave up her previous attempts to build a

[74] For an analysis of French attitudes toward the pact after its signing, see *ibid.*, pp. 262–267.

coalition against Hitler. Blum, as the Socialist Prime Minister of France, even went so far as to accept the British demand that France cease her aid to the Spanish Republic and declare her neutrality in the struggle.[75]

It is obvious that on the eve of the *Anschluss* and the Sudeten crisis efforts either to form a coalition against Hitler or to convert him to a system of brokerage had failed. The year 1938 opened with the West having no plans, either political or military, to meet the next German move. In addition both Italy and the Soviet Union had been lost as possible allies. It was this situation that made it possible for Hitler to achieve a dominant position in Eastern Europe and to level his penultimate blow at what remained of the Locarno balance.

Yet even with the diplomatic situation so much to his advantage, Hitler's moves into Eastern Europe in 1938 involved him in his greatest risk up to that date. As we have seen, the *Anschluss* depended for its success on Italian policy. But the Sudeten crisis not only brought him into frontal conflict with a state who was determined to fight back, unlike Austria, but also and even more dangerously, into a head-on confrontation with Britain. In doing so, Hitler for the first time managed to draw Britain into a direct concern with the affairs and boundaries of Eastern Europe.

How did Chamberlain attempt to meet this threat to the balance of power? First and foremost, he tried to continue the basic fundamentals of appeasement as it had been practiced by the British governments that had preceded him. Yet even before the Sudeten crisis Chamberlain had recognized the need for change in British diplomacy in an effort to make up for the failures of past policies and to improve the possibilities of successfully using appeasement. Thus, in early 1938 he made attempts to come to an agreement with Mussolini by liquidating the Spanish Civil War and thereby to draw Mussolini into at least a neutral posi-

[75] Furnia, *op. cit.,* pp. 209–210.

tion if not to the side of Britain and France. Second, it was largely under Chamberlain's inspiration and direction that Britain started to rearm as early as 1935 and to speed up rearmament as tensions increased. As we have seen, this program had a considerable measure of success by 1939, although there were immense defects, especially in the realm of military planning. It was because British military power was growing that during the Munich crisis some members of the German General Staff made an effort to work behind Hitler's back in collaboration with the British Government in order to stave off war.[76] Thus, Chamberlain was well aware of the need to apply coercion to Hitler as a crucial part of the policy of appeasement and had set in motion the machinery that would make such coercion possible. The third change that Chamberlain brought to the policy of appeasement was to recognize the need for a more sweeping modification in the balance established at Locarno than even the British had previously proposed. We have already discussed some of the problems and pitfalls the idea of such a change involved. There is little evidence that Chamberlain had reckoned with the complexity of such change, but that he intended to make a final settlement with Hitler by offering him a once-and-for-all large-scale bargain in Eastern Europe in return for Hitler's acceptance of a system of brokerage is clear from his conduct in the Sudeten crisis. In proposing this bargain Chamberlain was striving to maintain the balance of power; indeed, it was precisely because he was striving to maintain the balance that he proposed the bargain. All the changes that he had made in British policy were directed toward that end.

Yet there was ambiguity at the heart of this policy, the significance of which transcends this particular episode in

[76] For documentation on this episode, see E. L. Woodward and R. Butler, eds., *Documents on British Foreign Policy, 1919–1939* (London, 1946 ff.), 3d ser., Vol. II, pp. 683–692. For a judicious description of these efforts, see Wheeler-Bennett, *op. cit.,* pp. 404–424.

the history of the balance of power but which was plainly
and starkly revealed in the trend of British policy during
the crisis.

The ambiguity resulted from the newly established equilibrium of power achieved by Germany and lay in Chamberlain's acutely developed—too acutely, for he overestimated German power—sense of the high costs that might
result from the use of coercion against Hitler in order to
convert him to a system of brokerage. As Chamberlain
faced the fact of an equilibrium of power, he increasingly
saw the need to postpone the use of coercion against Hitler
until Britain was in a better military position. Thus, Britain
had to rely more and more on argument alone as a means
of converting Hitler. More than any other governmental
leader of Britain in this period, Chamberlain was aware
of the need for the existence and use of coercive force in
dealing with Hitler, but as the fact of equilibrium was
thrust upon him, he found himself less able to use that
force than had the leaders who had preceded him.

The existence of this ambiguity in Chamberlain's policy
is clearly evident in his thinking about the problems of British foreign policy in early 1938. In a speech at Birmingham
in April 1938, he could say that while Britain had no alternative but to go on with her rearmament program, there
"must be something in common" between Britain and Germany "if only we can find it," and that perhaps because of
Britain's "very aloofness from the rest of Europe we may
have some special part to play as conciliator and mediator"
in Europe's quarrels.[77] In private he also stated that "until
we are *fully* rearmed, our position must remain one of
great anxiety," and that Britain was "in no position to enter
light-heartedly upon war with such a formidable power as
Germany." [78] In the same letter he also said:

[77] K. Feiling, *The Life of Neville Chamberlain* (London, 1946),
p. 321.
[78] *Ibid.*, p. 323, private letter of January 16, 1938. Italics added.

I do not myself take too pessimistic a view of the situation. The dictators are too often regarded as though they were entirely inhuman. I believe this idea to be quite erroneous. It is indeed the human side of the dictators that makes them dangerous, but on the other hand, it is the side on which they can be approached with the greatest hope of successful issue.

I am about to enter upon a fresh attempt to reach a reasonable understanding with both Germany and Italy, and I am by no means unhopeful of getting results.[79]

Even after the *Anschluss,* when he thought that "it is perfectly evident, surely, now that force is the only argument Germany understands" and that "Heaven knows, I don't want to get back to alliances but if Germany continues to behave as she has done lately, she may drive us to it," he went on to state his belief that "if we can avoid another violent coup in Czechoslovakia, which ought to be feasible, it may be possible for Europe to settle down again, and some day for us to start peace talks with the Germans." [80] The type of deal he had in mind was a comprehensive one, as is shown by his comments on the visit of Lord Halifax to Hitler in late 1937.

The German visit was from my point of view a great success, because it achieved its object, that of creating an atmosphere in which it is possible to discuss with Germany the practical questions involved in a European settlement. . . . Both Hitler and Goering said separately, and emphatically, that they had no desire or intention of making war, and I think we may take this as correct, at any rate for the present. Of course, they want to dominate Eastern Europe; they want as close a union with Austria as they can get without incorporating her in the Reich, and they want much the same things for the Sudetendeutsche as we did for

[79] *Ibid.,* p. 324.
[80] *Ibid.,* pp. 341–342, March 13, 1938.

the Uitlanders in the Transvaal. They want Togoland and Kamerun. I am not quite sure where they stand about S. W. Africa; but they do not insist on Tanganyika, if they can be given some reasonably equivalent territory on the West Coast, possibly to be carved out of Belgian Congo and Angola. I think they would be prepared to come back to the League, if it were shorn of its compulsory powers, now clearly shown to be ineffective, and though Hitler was rather non-committal about disarmament, he did declare himself in favour of the abolition of bombing aeroplanes. Now here, it seems to me, is a fair basis of discussion, though no doubt all these points bristle with difficulties. But I don't see why we shouldn't say to Germany, "give us satisfactory assurances that you won't use force to deal with the Austrians and Czechoslovakians, and we will give you similar assurances that we won't use force to prevent the changes you want, if you can get them by peaceful means." [81]

Leaving aside the remarks on colonies, this is the Locarno idea writ large. As we have seen, Britain had always been willing to leave the door open to the peaceful expansion of Germany in Eastern Europe on the theory that as long as Britain was pledged to come to the aid of France in case of a German attack the balance would continue to exist. Chamberlain never backed away from his pledge to France, even though he was disgusted with the weaknesses of French political life and its leadership. But although Chamberlain's plans were the Locarno idea writ large, it is also necessary to recognize that it was Locarno writ very large indeed. It was the Locarno balance stretched almost to the breaking point.

But in Chamberlain's mind it would not break as long as the proviso about peaceful change was maintained. This was no empty figure of speech. To Chamberlain it represented the most significant demand that Britain had to make on Germany and the crucial element of the system

[81] *Ibid.*, pp. 332–333, November 26, 1937.

of brokerage in this particular situation as far as he was concerned. Peaceful change in Eastern Europe meant to Chamberlain that Germany was not to use her military machine to achieve power in that area because, first, it would activate the French treaty system with Poland and Czechoslovakia and hence quite possibly draw Britain into a war on the side of France, thus destroying the whole balance of power system by starting a major war. Second, and most important, the use of the German military machine in and of itself would create an instability—to put it mildly—that would make impossible the establishment of a system of brokerage by which Hitler would accept limits on his own aspiration within a balance. Hitler must recognize the demands of other powers, must recognize what they would *not* give him, and the crucial thing they would not give him was the right to the military conquest of other states in Europe. They would not do so, not only because of an affection for the rights of sovereign states—an affection that Chamberlain, like any statesman, possessed only to a limited degree—but more important because the use of the German Army in Eastern Europe would express Hitler's refusal to accept any limits, or, in other words, would express his refusal to accept the essence of brokerage. The German Army, therefore, should not be used as the means of expansion, for only in that case was there a chance of both satisfying some of Hitler's key objectives *and* erecting a system by which a new balance could be struck.[82]

It was in pursuit of this dual aim of giving the Sudetenland to Hitler while restricting the role of the German Army as the means by which Hitler should achieve that object that Chamberlain intervened in the Sudeten crisis.

[82] Medlicott, in "The Coming of the War in 1939," *op. cit.,* p. 237, describes Chamberlain's policy thus: "He was prepared in the last resort to acquiesce in the Nazi assimilation of Austria and even of the Sudeten German regions of Czechoslovakia if this came about by some 'peaceful process' and was to be the prelude to a genuine détente."

It was an intervention flawed from the beginning with Chamberlain's ambiguity about the role of coercive power in a condition of equilibrium.

Britain entered into the Sudeten crisis by taking upon herself the role of a broker in the most literal sense of the term through the Runciman mission, the object of which was to bring about an agreement between the Czech Government and the Sudeten Germans. On the surface it was an attempt to negotiate the dispute on its merits, but in fact it was an attempt to force the Czech Government to give large enough concessions in the form of autonomy to the Sudeten Germans so that they and Hitler—especially Hitler—would be satisfied. For even before the Runciman mission, and as early as March 1938, Chamberlain had recognized that there was no possibility of fighting in support of the Czech Government in order to preserve the unity of Czechoslovakia. Thus, on March 20, 1938, Chamberlain wrote privately about the possibility of resisting German demands for the Sudetenland:

. . . to be badgered and pressed to come out and give a clear, decided, bold, and unmistakable lead, show "ordinary courage" and all the rest of the twaddle, is calculated to vex the man who has to take the responsibility for the consequences. As a matter of fact, the plan of the "Grand Alliance," as Winston calls it, had occurred to me long before he mentioned it. . . . I talked about it to Halifax, and we submitted it to the Chiefs of Staff and the F.O. experts. It is a very attractive idea; indeed, there is almost everything to be said for it until you come to examine its practicability. From that moment its attraction vanishes. You have only to look at the map to see that nothing that France or we could do could possibly save Czechoslovakia from being overrun by the Germans, if they wanted to do it. The Austrian frontier is practically open; the great Skoda munition works are within easy bombing distance of the German aerodromes, the railways all pass through German territory, Russia is 100 miles away. Therefore we could not help Czechoslovakia—she would simply be a pretext for going to war with Germany. That we could not think of unless we had a reasonable prospect of being able to beat her to her knees in a reasonable time, and of that I see no sign. I have therefore abandoned any idea of giving guarantees to Czechoslovakia, or the French in connection with their obligations to that country.[83]

On March 24 Chamberlain made public the fundamental approach revealed in these remarks in a statement to Parliament on the Sudeten problem. He refused to guarantee Czechoslovakia because she was not a vital interest to Britain. However, he also attempted to give a warning to Germany, for he added that if war between Germany and Czechoslovakia occurred, "the inexorable pressure of facts might well prove more powerful than formal pronouncements" and that countries other than those originally involved might become engaged in such a war, namely Britain and France. The imprecision of this statement was calculated to deter the Germans;[84] the phrase about the "inexorable pressure of facts" also held the implication that Britain might come to the conclusion that in such a war she would have to fight to preserve the balance of power.

Because it was precisely such a conflict that Britain hoped to avoid, this statement created more problems for the British than it solved and in itself only sharpened the difficulty of keeping order in Eastern Europe without involving the disorder of war. The way in which the statement was to be used to influence Germany was candidly—and somewhat optimistically—explained in a letter from Halifax, foreign secretary of Britain at the time, to Henderson, British ambassador to Berlin and one of the most ardent appeasers, on August 5, 1938, when the Runciman mission was beginning its work in Czechoslovakia. Halifax lays down the brokerage roles that he expects Britain, and

[82] Feiling, *op. cit.*, pp. 347–348.
[84] Eubank, *op. cit.*, p. 36.

hopes Hitler, will play. In doing so, he reveals clearly the ambiguity of British policy.

We cannot I suppose judge with certainty of what may be German intentions. I find it difficult to believe that, *if they were convinced it meant a general war,* they would think it worth while to try and insist by force on their full desiderata for Czechoslovakia, whatever these may be. Indeed I would have guessed that if they were so convinced, they would in fact find means of putting up, with good or ill grace, with a great deal less. And it is on this no doubt that Beneš or those behind him are tempted to count.

I should judge therefore that in all German policy at this time there was a strong element of bluff, in the sense that calling up of reservists, Eastern [sic] fortifications, bellicose speeches, etc., were all calculated to make us feel that they were ready to go to war, and that therefore we on our side should hesitate to bluff, and still less to take military action against them. . . .

All this is not to say that the Germans may not be planning the worst. There is a good deal of evidence to show that a party at least is. Still less does it prove that if there was the "bloodbath" among the S.D. [Sudeten Deutsche], Hitler would or could not hold his hand, whatever the cost. But it does suggest the importance of our holding as firmly as we can to our line of (as John Buchan put it to me the other day) perpetually telling Beneš of what we might *not* do in the event of trouble: and of tactfully reminding the Germans of what we *might* do. And meanwhile use every effort to coerce the two sides, by joint pressure and persuasion, into agreement. . . .

Supposing the worst happens. The French will presumably mobilize, unless indeed the Czechs have so behaved as to warrant the French saying they have been eminently unreasonable and therefore doing nothing. I should doubt:

   (a) the French attacking the Siegfried line,
   (b) the Germans attacking France.

And in one form or another, I should have guessed that

there would have been talking; after the Germans had created a situation in which they would have made it very difficult, except after imposing on them defeat through general war, to maintain the present situation unchanged. And I have always felt that to fight a war for 1, 2, or 3 years to protect or recreate something that you knew you could not directly protect, and probably could never recreate, did not make sense.

But that feeling should not prevent us, or you, from constantly repeating March 24 warnings, and doing our utmost to get it into the very stupid heads of the Germans that if they insisted on stepping on the spring, the gun was awfully likely to go off. It is our only chance as I see it of preventing them doing it, and it is a difficult line to ride, without exposing ourselves to humiliation if we don't go to war. And that, with you, I have no intention of doing over Czechoslovakia if I can avoid it. France is obviously a different matter, and I have always presumed that this difference is as present to the German mind as it is to ours.

Therefore, I come back to the line of March 24, which I am sure is right, and nothing that any of us ever say or do ought to give any tittle of encouragement to the Germans to believe that the danger of British intervention is negligible.[85]

Such were the plans. But between the time this dispatch was written and the first meeting of Chamberlain with Hitler at Berchtesgaden (September 15), the debacle of this approach had set in, and the failure of Chamberlain's effort to establish a system of brokerage with Hitler was demonstrated. As we have seen, both Chamberlain and Halifax were aware of the need to threaten war if Hitler went "too far." And, in fact, after Chamberlain's second meeting with Hitler at Godesberg (September 22), the British essentially broke off negotiations, withdrew from their efforts to establish a system of brokerage, and began to prepare for war because it was at this conference that

[85] DBFP, 3d ser., Vol. II, Doc. 587. Italics in original.

Hitler refused to be content with the acquisition of the Sudetenland as already agreed upon by the British, but insisted that German troops occupy it immediately. This demand was too much for Chamberlain to accept, for it raised precisely the issue upon which he was adamant, that the expansion of German power into Eastern Europe should be through negotiation and not through German military power. To break off negotiations on this question was no higgling over a detail for Chamberlain; his insistence on this condition was an effort to retain some last shred of brokerage through the pretense that German military power was restrained, limited, and controlled. This was the high moment of the Munich crisis, when it seemed that all hope had gone and war was inevitable. Europe was temporarily saved from war by Hitler's dramatic and last-minute step back from the precipice with his letter to Chamberlain offering to negotiate the details of the take-over of the Sudetenland. Hitler suddenly seemed to accept the broker's role offered to him by Chamberlain as a result of the British threat to go to war if he did not do so. But, in fact, since Chamberlain had already offered him the Sudetenland for full and complete incorporation into Germany at Berchtesgaden and since Britain's attempt to achieve autonomy for the Sudetenland within the Czech state had failed, Hitler was once again using a pseudo-broker's role in order to achieve his objectives. At the Munich Conference (September 29) Hitler got everything he wanted, including military occupation, give or take a few details to assuage the susceptibilities of the British Prime Minister.

Munich revealed the ambiguity that lay at the heart of Chamberlain's appeasement policy, his recognition of the

[86] To discuss other sources of this reluctance would take us outside the framework of this study. It can be said here, however, that it was also the result of a concern over the economic effects on Britain of rearmament and military conflict, the influence of the pro-German opinions of much of the Tory Party, and a sincere horror of military conflict.

need to apply coercion yet his profound reluctance to use it[86] in view of the military equilibrium that had been achieved by Hitler. Munich has become a synonym for retreat, yet if there was Munich, there was Godesberg before it, when Chamberlain finally turned his back momentarily on one-sided concessions and prepared for war; it was, after all, these preparations for war on the part of Britain that created the crisis of Munich. Chamberlain's ambiguity at this juncture could hardly be more graphically portrayed than in the contrast between Godesberg and Munich. He seized the excuse of Hitler's acceptance of a pseudobroker's role because Chamberlain's ambiguity about the use of military power made it impossible for him to face the consequences of war without one more attempt to establish a system of brokerage without the use of coercion.

The Balance and the Holder of the Balance

Putting Munich in the larger context of British policy in the 1930's makes it possible to answer the question posed earlier, namely, what light does the failure of appeasement throw on the lag in adjusting to a new balance of power situation on the part of those states whose aim was to defend the balance? As we have seen, the question arises from the whole nature of British policy in these years, which was to pursue the making of another Locarno until 1938, when Britain was in a poor position to pursue anything else. The diplomacy of Britain in this period shows a high degree of consistency with her policy in the 1920's, when by all the rules of the balance of power it should have demonstrated change. For Britain as the holder of the balance should have functioned in the 1930's to maintain the balance through the active exercise of her role as a balancer. The active exercise of that role would have meant the use of British power in support of France before 1938 in order to bring about a preponderance of power on one side of the balance and thus prevent Germany from operating in such a way as to destroy the balance. Britain, precisely because she was the holder of the balance, should have chosen sides in these years, in contrast to the 1920's, and made up whatever deficiencies existed in her military capabilities to ensure that there was a preponderance of power on one side. Then she could have done what she attempted but failed to achieve, namely, to force Hitler into a system of brokerage. By 1938 Chamberlain was moving toward such a policy, but by then it was too late for Britain to effectively perform this role except at the heavy cost of a major war, which was in itself a sign of the failure of the holder of the balance to maintain the balance. The stickiness in the way the holder of the balance functioned in this era is made manifest in Britain's consistent attempt to act as a go-between between France and Germany rather than to act on the side of France, and in doing so to force Hitler to accept the role of a broker. A study of British diplomacy in the 1930's is a study of the holder of the balance, which makes it possible to draw some conclusions about the nature of this role.

1. The diplomatic events of this period demonstrate a potential weakness in the way in which a holder of the balance performs his role. If a holder of the balance has significant and vital interests to protect outside the area in which the particular balance is established, a dualism in his foreign policy can and probably will arise. This dualism will exert what might be called a centrifugal force on the holder, which drags him away from his involvement in the balance of which he is the holder. These outside interests will either divert the holder from his concern with that balance or will bring about conflicts that cut across the alignments within the balance, thus weakening it. In the 1930's Britain accepted her losses at the hands of Japan in the Far East because to make the necessary effort in that area would have weakened her so drastically in Europe

that she would no longer have been in a position to play the role of the holder of the balance. But the Ethiopian crisis and the Spanish Civil War faced her with a cruel choice. What was at question in both cases was a threat to Britain's control of the Mediterranean Sea through the rise of Italian power in the area. Rightly or wrongly Britain accepted the challenge, although in a half-hearted way. The result was the alienation of Italy, the consummation of Italian-German friendship,[87] and the creation of opportunities on the continent for Hitler.

As a holder of the balance, Britain had allowed interests and problems that were peripheral to the balance to distract her and to confuse the political situation on the continent. In doing so she failed to carry out her function of manipulating the states of Europe and the relationships between them in order to maximize the effectiveness of the balance of power. For it is this function that the holder must perform and for which the role is designed. He plays his role in a situation in which other states have relatively little or no freedom of maneuver. He, however, can manipulate them by his influence, which rests both on his power and his freedom from commitment; he can both coerce and make offers to other states because he is not irrevocably tied to any one state or group of states and hence determines where preponderance will lie. To come into conflict, however, with one of the states in a balance over an issue that is not vital to the balance can essentially negate the position of the holder, since such a conflict can create alliances that make it impossible for the weight of the holder to bring about a preponderance of power if it is thrown on one side; the result is to force the holder himself increasingly to one side of the balance merely to bring about an equilibrium. Britain's conflict with Italy over the

[87] For some information on the conflict within the British Government over this question, see I. Colvin, *None So Blind: A British Diplomatic View of the Origins of World War II* (New York, 1965), Ch. IV.

Mediterranean area was of this nature and essentially destroyed her position as a holder of the balance.

2. The experience of Britain in these years indicates that the relationship between the domestic political system of a holder of the balance to his foreign policies may pose a problem that is unique to the holder. The domestic political system of a holder may see this particular role as one that enables low costs to be paid for the involvements of foreign policy and that will enable the state to adopt a quasi-isolationist policy of intervention only in certain crucial areas and at certain crucial episodes or times. Rather than seeing the state as actively and continuously engaged in the affairs of a balance, it may view her as somewhat detached and playing a waiting role. The holder of the balance would be correctly conceived not only or merely as a status quo power, but as a status quo power that is not fundamentally at odds with any particular state or set of states. But the domestic political system may, therefore, feel itself free to engage in bouts of moralizing about the world and to stand relatively aloof from specific conflicts. The demands that it imposes on its leaders are those that tend to minimize the use of force against other states and to maximize the role of an impartial go-between. In such a situation appeasement, with a minimum of coercive power supporting it, is probably the most active policy feasible. Any other active policy would destroy this particular image of the holder and require another concept of the role of the state to be presented to and accepted by the domestic political system. This is not impossible, obviously, but it requires a broker who is aware of the need for change and who is in a position to make such a change.

Britain's political system during the 1930's put forth demands that made it difficult for her to create and use coercive force against Germany. British public opinion, insofar as it manifested itself, either demonstrated a desire for isolationism or struck moral stances (as in the

Ethiopian crisis and the Spanish Civil War) in support of the League of Nations, with the Labor Party leading the way.[88] Against these forces were those who were advocates of appeasement because they could see no need for a change in Britain's policies as a holder since they had been so successful in the past and since they were so inexpensive; they centered themselves in such venerable institutions as *The Times* and All Souls[89] or in strategic niches of upper-class society and the Tory Party. The reality of the threat posed by Hitler's Germany did not break through to the domestic political system of Britain until the Munich crisis, when it was too late. Except among a minority, the demand the British political system made upon its brokers, and through them on the international system, was only that the balance should be adjusted to rectify the wrongs produced by the Versailles Treaty. It was Chamberlain's greatest failure, and that of Baldwin before him, that they did not tell the domestic system that this was no longer the issue. They did not do so because they fundamentally agreed with the basic postulate put forth by the system, that a holder of the balance should be able to perform his duties without involvement or significant commitment to one or the other of those who were quarreling on the continent. The appeasement policy of Baldwin and Chamberlain was the only form of active foreign policy that the British political system would find acceptable at this time, and even it had to labor under the attacks of those who preferred moral gestures of isolation.

Yet over a period of time Baldwin and Chamberlain both sought with some considerable success to modify the demand put forward by the domestic political system in order to achieve a significant degree of rearmament. But

[88] See A. J. P. Taylor, *English History, 1914–1945* (New York, 1965), pp. 413–414, for the confusions in the Labor Party on the issue of rearmament.

[89] See A. L. Rouse, *Appeasement, A Study in Political Decline, 1933–1939* (New York, 1963), for a description of the political atmosphere at All Souls in the years of appeasement.

the lag in this achievement as well as in changing the
policy it was supposed to underpin was due in part to the
concept of the holder held by the domestic political system. In contrast, the French domestic system, disorganized
though it was in the vital years 1934–1936, was able to
support a policy of continental alliance against Hitler.
However, because by definition France was one of the
two opposing states in the balance, it lacked the ability to
cope with German power unless Britain as the holder of
the balance placed herself on the French side. Hence,
France was dependent on the course of British policy.

Manifestly, a lag in the adjustment of the domestic
political system to a new balance of power situation need
not occur. But the experience of Britain in the 1930's indicates that these systems are at the very least susceptible to
such a lag because of the expectations of the domestic
political system about this role.

3. The most important source of lag in the adjustment
of a balance to the new situation created by risktakers
such as Hitler is the threat that this adjustment possesses
for the holder of the balance. As we have seen, in the
process of trying to discipline a risktaker such as Hitler to
work within a system of brokerage it may be necessary
to come down on one side of the balance in order to establish a preponderance of power. Yet, in doing so the
holder of the balance will destroy the special position and
privileges that have been achieved by remaining unattached
to both sides. A state, such as Britain, who has long been
unattached may find it difficult to make this change.

She will especially find it difficult to make this change
if she is called upon to do so at an early stage in the activities of a risktaker. Because risktakers will reject the
whole framework of brokerage if coercion is not applied
when the defenders of the balance hold a preponderance
of power, the system must apply coercion very early to a
risktaker and before he has created a base from which he
can establish an equilibrium of power. The defenders of

a balance must, therefore, take action on relatively minor infractions of the balance at a time when the threat is ambiguous. This early recognition and action is always difficult for any state to make. It is especially difficult for a holder of the balance because he seeks to maintain his position as long as possible.

The policy of Britain in the 1930's is one of the typical reactions of a holder of the balance to the type of situation created by Hitler. From the point of view of the holder of the balance, appeasement was a rational method of trying to *put off action* and to seek out the terms on which a modification of the balance might satisfy German demands without causing Britain to lose her special position of a noncommitted state. There was, of course, much foolishness in British policy, much that was based on a simpleminded pro-Germanism among many members of Britain's ruling classes and an incredible degree of naiveté among all walks of political life from King Edward VIII down to the lowliest Labor Party ward worker. But there was more behind the policy of appeasement than prejudice and stupidity, a fact that has been obscured by the analysis of appeasement simply as a study in prejudice and stupidity.

Britain was unwilling to throw her weight on one side of the balance at the very first sign of Hitler's risktaking because to do so would threaten Britain not only with the possibility of armed conflict but with the loss of the special advantages she had derived from the particular way she had played her role as a holder of the balance. To maintain those particular advantages as long as possible was in Britain's self-interest, for it provided her with influence among all the states of the continent, freed her for the pursuit of her interests outside Europe, and made it possible to avoid a permanent commitment to either of the two blocs at conflict within Europe. Her particular view of how the holder should behave gave Britain a unique position of freedom above the two contending sides and a freedom of maneuver that not only increased and maxi-

mized her choice of policy and protected her from the
heavy costs of direct involvement, but also increased her
value to other states. Playing her role as a holder of the
balance as she did, Britain was the kingpin and the master
of Europe. And all this with a relatively small output of
military energy on her part. It is no wonder that Chamberlain inveighed so bitterly against the French policy of
alliances, since such a policy threatened to bring Britain's
freedom to an end.

It is obvious that a holder of the balance should be
willing to threaten his own privileges by lining up on one
side of the balance at the first sign of an infraction of the
balance. The experience of Britain in the 1930's makes it
clear that the interests of the holder in being noncommitted
to either of the two states in direct conflict would at the
very least inhibit such an action and make his willingness
to sacrifice his advantages sticky, slow, and sluggish. Appeasement as practiced by Chamberlain and other foreign
secretaries in the 1930's was a way of avoiding such a
sacrifice, and hence may be seen as a typical policy of a
holder of the balance when faced by a risktaker. The
French were much more willing to engage in a policy of
alliances and coercion than the British precisely because
they were in direct confrontation with Germany rather
than in the position of a holder of the balance; they failed,
because after 1925 they had relied to such a degree on
the protection afforded to them by the holder of the balance that they lacked the means to act on their own.

Before 1938 Britain and France taken together could
have provided a preponderance of power if the structure
of the balance had not been so closely interwoven with the
British concept of Britain's role as the holder of the balance. For Britain to have acted in such a way as to create
that preponderance before 1938 would have struck at the
roots of Britain's concept of that role. It would take a
series of decisive events to force her to play the role in a
different way. But by then it would be too late to save

the balance. The holder of the balance had taken too long to realize that a change in her own concept of the balance was needed, that the holder of the balance would have to come down on one side of the balance in order to establish the preponderance of power that would coerce a risktaker such as Hitler. The diplomacy of the 1930's indicates that if a holder of the balance has acquired a special position of relative freedom and detachment within a balance of power system, he may be reluctant to give up those advantages and to adopt another form of the role. He will thereby cause a lag in the adjustment of the balance of power to new situations.

Chapter Four

Conclusion: The Struggle for the Balance of Power

The failure to use power in the 1930's to create a balance of power and thus to check Hitler was the failure of a particular time and not the failure of the balance as a method of operation in international relations. It is illegitimate to conclude from that failure that the balance of power has ceased to be an effective instrument of order and stability. Instead, the evidence substantiates the idea that the principle of the balance could have been used as an effective method of restraint against Hitler, that even though Hitler and Nazi Germany were extreme cases of threats to the balance of power they could have been limited in their expansionist drives by the use of counter-power. This conclusion—the Churchillian "unnecessary war" thesis—is detailed by the evidence released since the end of the war, showing what a "damned close-run thing" (to use the Duke of Wellington's phrase) it was in the 1930's.

It is all the more necessary, therefore, to understand why the balance was not used effectively. For the evidence of these years also demonstrates the difficulties of using the balance of power as a means of creating or preserving order when the balance is threatened by a risktaker. The difficulties are those of timing and the need for early action, of the right proportions of appeasement and coercion, and of the choices that must be made by that power or those powers that possess preponderant power, especially when they are the holder of the balance as in the case of Britain. It is more useful to see the failure of appeasement in these terms rather than only in terms of the personal failings of those who held power at that time. By shifting the emphasis away from the foolishness or wickedness or fears of an individual or a group and putting it on the problems of maintaining or creating a balance in such an epoch we are able to learn something about the problem of using the balance of power to cope with a risktaker.

In the struggle for a balance—"for" in the sense of both keeping or seeking a balance—the crucial problems that must be faced revolve around the difficulties of changing the balance of power to meet new and different threats to stability and, of equal importance, new and different conditions and demands. The need for such change arises from shifts of a potentially expansive state along the continuum that runs between the broker at one end and the risktaker at the other. As a result of these shifts, the relative proportions of appeasement and coercion must change, not, unfortunately, in a simple one-to-one ratio, but in a complex way that will satisfy the needs created by a complex situation. It is as important to realize that the degree of appeasement may need to be increased in particular situations and in dealing with particular states as it is to realize that the degree of coercion must be increased in other situations and in dealing with other states, since otherwise the balance of power will be identified with a status quo conservatism that will lead to the creation of more tension and instability rather than less. Locarno is a case where appeasement created a stable balance because the state who aimed at expansion was willing to use brokerage as a way of achieving her objective and hence was willing to work within the balance of power. The 1930's is an extreme case of the opposite nature. But some degree of coercion and appeasement was necessary in both cases.

In our consideration of the diplomacy of the 1930's we have seen some of the difficulties of making a change in the balance of power to meet the problem of a new situation. One of these difficulties is to identify the new situation and the type of state who is putting forth demands on the defenders of the balance, to determine whether she is closer to one or the other end of the continuum. To a very large extent this identification can only come about through a process of trial and error, a process that takes time and, hence, may make the proper timing impossible, for by the time the identification has been made, the moment for action may have passed. Contrariwise, however, a too early identification on inadequate grounds may lead to a mistaken policy and create a type of enemy who would not otherwise have existed. Given the complexities of real situations and of the forces at work on individual leaders, it is clear that even this first and elementary step in bringing about change in a balance of power is extremely difficult to make. It becomes, therefore, easier and more tempting *not* to change, to postulate into the future what has been in the past. The inability of the British in particular to understand correctly the problem of Hitler demonstrates this problem, for they wildly either underestimated or overestimated his aims or power. Their ability to make those changes that were necessary, if the balance was to continue to be an effective instrument of restraint, was vitiated at the very source. That the task is difficult and that, therefore, there was good reason for their failure did not make it any less disastrous.

But even given the proper identification of a state, the next step in bringing about a change in the balance is equally difficult to take. The cost of change on the part of those states who seek to defend the balance can be so great that they may inhibit the changes that are necessary.

Those costs are of two varieties. First are those costs that
are the direct result of either appeasement or coercion,
of either giving up territory or influence in order to appease or building up armaments in order to coerce. These
costs, obviously, can be considerable; in the 1930's the
costs of rearmament were seen to be so heavy that it was
felt to be desirable to avoid them as long as there were
other alternatives. Hence, alternatives were sought as long
as possible. The result was Britain's policy of perpetuating
the Locarno balance unchanged or with as little modification as was feasible. Even the French, avidly anti-German
though they were, sought to minimize the cost of rearm-
ing against Germany through a policy of static defense.
It must not be forgotten, of course, that both states and
especially Britain were staggering under tremendous economic crises in the 1930's and that to add to their economic
woes by a heavy burden of rearmament was seen at that
time to be political as well as economic suicide.

There is, however, another category of costs to be paid
if the balance is to be changed, those that result from
downgrading or ignoring other foreign policy objectives
in order to preserve the balance of power *as a system*.
To maintain a given balance of power, choices may have
to be made to use the limited resources of a state in such
a way that sacrifices are required of certain interests of the
state that do not bear directly on the balance of power.
We have seen that Britain made such a sacrifice in the
Far East in the early 1930's but that she could not bring
herself to do so in the Mediterranean area in the middle
1930's, and we have also seen the result of that refusal.
The concentration of policy and means required to maintain a balance may well lead to a totally different foreign
policy from that which would be involved in the pursuit
of national interests as such. It may also and most probably
will lead to a conflict between national interests defined traditionally and outside the context of a balance of power
and the policy that is the logical result of a struggle for

the balance of power. The former have a "concreteness," a "specificity," that the more abstract idea of the balance lacks. Hence, immediate interests may overcome the more general interest of supporting a balance. That such a conflict occurred in the realm of British policy in the 1930's is evidenced not only by the Ethiopian affair but also by the Anglo-German Naval Pact, in which Britain pursued a particular interest to the detriment of the balance of power as a whole.

A variant of this problem of bringing about change in a balance is the need to assume new responsibilities in order to preserve a balance. These may be quite far removed from a direct interest of a defender of the balance; they may be interests that are crucial to some states in the balance and of no special concern to the other states in the balance. Yet unless this burden is accepted as a new and vital aspect of a state's foreign policy, the balance may collapse. Especially significant in this respect is Britain's refusal to adopt a position of engagement toward Eastern Europe. While the hopes of Austen Chamberlain in the 1920's had some considerable basis even at that time, there was an ambiguity about British policy in this area, a doubt as to how far Britain would let Germany expand in the East and what controls she could and would put upon that expansion. Such ambiguity became disastrous after Hitler came to power. Only in 1938 did the British finally realize what Eastern Europe meant to the balance of power, but by then it was too late. It is both ironical and fitting that the British finally declared war on Germany after Germany attacked Poland. Eastern Europe was, in fact, a vital area to the balance of power, yet from the very beginning of the interwar era, in 1919 at the Paris Peace Conference, it was clearly seen as not being a vital interest, or indeed, of any interest, to the British. Allowing German expansion in Eastern Europe was a workable policy at least until 1933 and could have led to a new or modified balance if it were under control. But making it a controlled expansion would have meant the adoption by Britain of a commitment of some kind to Eastern Europe. One can understand British reluctance to enter into that cauldron of passionate and continuous conflict; one must also record the results and the meaning of those results. A policy that was vital to the balance of power was neglected in favor of policies in support of traditional national interests.

The struggle for the balance of power requires the constant invention of new policies, many of which will be unconcerned with traditional national interests, with the object of maintaining or creating a balance as such. The need for change is, therefore, a crucial aspect of balance of power politics, but the high costs of change make the balance sticky and sluggish in response to new conditions. A judgment on the balance of power as a method of bringing about some degree of order and stability in international relations must be made in the context of the difficulties of such change. What might be called the care and nurture of the balance of power as a system of order requires constant movement back and forth within the two ends of a continuum symbolized by Locarno on the one hand and the 1930's on the other. Given the nature of balance of power politics since the watershed of 1933, that movement will presumably take place closer to one end of the continuum than to the other; risktakers have become one of the facts of international life. But the fact that risktakers will vary in nature and intransigence means that even within the context of the change that has occurred since 1933 in international relations a mere reversal of the pattern of British and French policy in the 1930's will not suffice in the struggle for the balance of power. Even given the pursuit of a balance of power as a policy, change is required to meet different kinds of risktakers and threats to the balance. A study of the interwar years in general, and of the 1930's in particular, does not demonstrate what particular policy should be followed; it does not demonstrate that to follow a mirror-image of Chamberlain's Munich policy will always suffice for our era, that it is constantly necessary to do what Britain did not do in the 1930's. Rather, such a study demonstrates the difficulties and complexities of the decisions involved in using the balance of power as a means of regulating, restricting, and controlling the activities of an extreme risktaker such as Hitler. The problem the experience of the 1930's has posed ever since that time is whether the balance of power can successfully be used to deal with a Hitler, or with variations of the type of risktaker he personifies, without paying the costs involved in a major war such as World War II— costs so great that they render the balance useless as a way of establishing at least a degree of order in international relations. The evidence presented in this study indicates that the balance can be an effective restraint on such risktakers if it is an objective of policy as such, if other foreign and domestic interests are sacrificed to it, and if the defenders of the balance are willing and make it known that they are willing to pay the costs, military and otherwise, of maintaining the system before the risktaker can effectively threaten total war. But the evidence also makes clear that a risktaker such as Hitler can create a situation in which those states who would use the balance of power as a system of order are faced with unique problems as compared with an era in which such risktakers are absent. The failure of Britain and France in the 1930's was a failure to recognize that the Locarno era had come to an end and that different problems and different methods were required if the balance was to be maintained as a system. The uniqueness of those problems did not and does not mean that the balance is useless in such a situation; it does mean that given the presence of a Hitler or of a state with similar characteristics, the manipulation of power necessary to maintain the balance must take special forms.

(1) Final Protocol of the Locarno Conference, 1925 (Translation)

The representatives of the German, Belgian, British, French, Italian, Polish, and Czechoslovak Governments, who have met at Locarno from the 5th to 16th October, 1925, in order to seek by common agreement means for preserving their respective nations from the scourge of war and for providing for the peaceful settlement of disputes of every nature which might eventually arise between them.

Have given their approval to the draft treaties and conventions which respectively affect them and which, framed in the course of the present conference, are mutually interdependent:—

Treaty Between Germany, Belgium, France, Great Britain, and Italy (Annex A).

Arbitration Convention Between Germany and Belgium (Annex B).

Arbitration Convention Between Germany and France (Annex C).

[1] From Royal Institute of International Affairs, *Survey of International Affairs, 1925* (London, 1928), Vol. 2, pp. 439–452.

Arbitration Treaty Between Germany and Poland (Annex D).
Arbitration Treaty Between Germany and Czechoslovakia
  (Annex E).

These instruments, hereby initialed *ne varietur,* will bear
to-day's date, the representatives of the interested parties
agreeing to meet in London on the 1st December next, to
proceed during the course of a single meeting to the formality of the signature of the instruments which affect them.

The Minister for Foreign Affairs of France states that as
a result of the draft arbitration treaties mentioned above,
France, Poland, and Czechoslovakia have also concluded at
Locarno draft agreements in order reciprocally to assure
to themselves the benefit of the said treaties. These agree-
ments will be duly deposited at the League of Nations, but
M. Briand holds copies forthwith at the disposal of the
Powers represented here.

The Secretary of State for Foreign Affairs of Great Britain proposes that, in reply to certain requests for explanations concerning article 16 of the Covenant of the League of
Nations presented by the Chancellor and the Minister for
Foreign Affairs of Germany, a letter, of which the draft is
similarly attached (Annex F) should be addressed to them
at the same time as the formality of signature of the above-
mentioned instruments takes place. This proposal is agreed
to.

The representatives of the Governments represented here
declare their firm conviction that the entry into force of
these treaties and conventions will contribute greatly to bring
about a moral relaxation of the tension between nations,
that it will help powerfully towards the solution of many
political or economic problems in accordance with the
interests and sentiments of peoples, and that, in strengthening peace and security in Europe, it will hasten on effectively the disarmament provided for in article 8 of the
Covenant of the League of Nations.

They undertake to give their sincere co-operation to the
work relating to disarmament already undertaken by the
League of Nations and to seek the realization thereof in a
general agreement.

Done at Locarno, the 16th October, 1925.

> LUTHER.
> STRESEMANN.
> EMILE VANDERVELDE.
> ARI. BRIAND.
> AUSTEN CHAMBERLAIN.
> BENITO MUSSOLINI.
> AL. SKRZYNSKI.
> EDUARD BENES.

(2) Annex A: Treaty of Mutual Guarantee Between Germany, Belgium, France, Great Britain, and Italy (Translation)

The President of the German Reich, His Majesty the King of the Belgians, the President of the French Republic, and His Majesty the King of the United Kingdom of Great Britain and Ireland and of the British Dominions beyond the Seas, Emperor of India, His Majesty the King of Italy;

Anxious to satisfy the desire for security and protection which animates the peoples upon whom fell the scourge of the war of 1914–18;

Taking note of the abrogation of the treaties for the neutralization of Belgium, and conscious of the necessity of ensuring peace in the area which has so frequently been the scene of European conflicts;

Animated also with the sincere desire of giving to all the signatory Powers concerned supplementary guarantees within the framework of the Covenant of the League of Nations and the treaties in force between them;

Have determined to conclude a treaty with these objects, and have appointed as their plenipotentiaries: [names omitted]

Who, having communicated their full powers, found in good and due form, have agreed as follows:—

Article 1. The high contracting parties collectively and severally guarantee, in the manner provided in the following articles, the maintenance of the territorial *status quo* resulting from the frontiers between Germany and Belgium and between Germany and France and the inviolability of the said frontiers as fixed by or in pursuance of the Treaty of Peace signed at Versailles on the 28th June, 1919, and also the observance of the stipulations of articles 42 and 43 of the said treaty concerning the demilitarized zone.

Article 2. Germany and Belgium, and also Germany and France, mutually undertake that they will in no case attack or invade each other or resort to war against each other.

This stipulation shall not, however, apply in the case of—

1. The exercise of the right of legitimate defence, that is to say, resistance to a violation of the undertaking contained in the previous paragraph or to a flagrant breach of articles 42 or 43 of the said Treaty of Versailles, if such breach constitutes an unprovoked act of aggression and by reason of the assembly of armed forces in the demilitarized zone immediate action is necessary.

2. Action in pursuance of article 16 of the Covenant of the League of Nations.

3. Action as the result of a decision taken by the Assembly or by the Council of the League of Nations or in pursuance of article 15, paragraph 7, of the Covenant of the League of Nations, provided that in this last event the action is directed against a State which was the first to attack.

Article 3. In view of the undertakings entered into in article 2 of the present treaty, Germany and Belgium and Germany and France undertake to settle by peaceful means and in the manner laid down herein all questions of every kind which may arise between them and which it may not be possible to settle by the normal methods of diplomacy:

Any question with regard to which the parties are in conflict as to their respective rights shall be submitted to judicial decision, and the parties undertake to comply with such decision.

All other questions shall be submitted to a conciliation

commission. If the proposals of this commission are not accepted by the two parties, the question shall be brought before the Council of the League of Nations, which will deal with it in accordance with article 15 of the Covenant of the League.

The detailed arrangements for effecting such peaceful settlement are the subject of special agreements signed this day.

Article 4. (1) If one of the high contracting parties alleges that a violation of article 2 of the present treaty or a breach of articles 42 or 43 of the Treaty of Versailles has been or is being committed, it shall bring the question at once before the Council of the League of Nations.

(2) As soon as the Council of the League of Nations is satisfied that such violation or breach has been committed, it will notify its finding without delay to the Powers signatory of the present treaty, who severally agree that in such case they will each of them come immediately to the assistance of the Power against whom the act complained of is directed.

(3) In case of a flagrant violation of article 2 of the present treaty or of a flagrant breach of articles 42 or 43 of the Treaty of Versailles by one of the high contracting parties, each of the other contracting parties hereby undertakes immediately to come to the help of the party against whom such a violation or breach has been directed as soon as the said Power has been able to satisfy itself that this violation constitutes an unprovoked act of aggression and that by reason either of the crossing of the frontier or of the outbreak of hostilities or of the assembly of armed forces in the demilitarized zone immediate action is necessary. Nevertheless, the Council of the League of Nations, which will be seized of the question in accordance with the first paragraph of this article, will issue its findings, and the high contracting parties undertake to act in accordance with the recommendations of the Council provided that they are concurred in by all the members other than the representatives of the parties which have engaged in hostilities.

Article 5.   The provisions of article 3 of the present treaty are placed under the guarantee of the high contracting parties as provided by the following stipulations:—

If one of the Powers referred to in article 3 refuses to submit a dispute to peaceful settlement or to comply with an arbitral or judicial decision and commits a violation of article 2 of the present treaty or a breach of articles 42 or 43 of the Treaty of Versailles, the provisions of article 4 shall apply.

Where one of the Powers referred to in article 3, without committing a violation of article 2 of the present treaty or a breach of articles 42 or 43 of the Treaty of Versailles, refuses to submit a dispute to peaceful settlement or to comply with an arbitral or judicial decision, the other party shall bring the matter before the Council of the League of Nations, and the Council shall propose what steps shall be taken; the high contracting parties shall comply with these proposals.

Article 6.   The provisions of the present treaty do not affect the rights and obligations of the high contracting parties under the Treaty of Versailles or under arrangements supplementary thereto, including the agreements signed in London on the 30th August, 1924.

Article 7.   The present treaty, which is designed to ensure the maintenance of peace, and is in conformity with the Covenant of the League of Nations, shall not be interpreted as restricting the duty of the League to take whatever action may be deemed wise and effectual to safeguard the peace of the world.

Article 8.   The present treaty shall be registered at the League of Nations in accordance with the Covenant of the League. It shall remain in force until the Council, acting on a request of one or other of the high contracting parties notified to the other signatory Powers three months in advance, and voting at least by a two-thirds majority, decides that the League of Nations ensures sufficient protection to the high contracting parties; the treaty shall cease to have effect on the expiration of a period of one year from such a decision.

Article 9.   The present treaty shall impose no obligation upon any of the British dominions, or upon India, unless the Government of such dominion, or of India, signifies its acceptance thereof.

Article 10.   The present treaty shall be ratified and the ratifications shall be deposited at Geneva in the archives of the League of Nations as soon as possible.

It shall enter into force as soon as all the ratifications have been deposited and Germany has become a member of the League of Nations.

The present treaty, done in a single copy, will be deposited in the archives of the League of Nations, and the Secretary-General will be requested to transmit certified copies to each of the high contracting parties.

In faith whereof the above-mentioned plenipotentiaries have signed the present treaty.

Done at Locarno, the 16th October, 1925.

> LUTHER.
> STRESEMANN.
> EMILE VANDERVELDE.
> A. BRIAND.
> AUSTEN CHAMBERLAIN.
> BENITO MUSSOLINI.

(3) Annexes B and C: Arbitration Conventions Between Germany and Belgium and Between Germany and France[2] (Translation)

The undersigned duly authorized.

Charged by their respective Governments to determine the methods by which, as provided in article 3 of the treaty concluded this day between Germany, Belgium, France, Great Britain, and Italy, a peaceful solution shall be at-

---

[2] The terms of these two conventions are identical.

tained of all questions which cannot be settled amicably between Germany and Belgium,

Have agreed as follows:—

Part I

Article 1.   All disputes of every kind between Germany and Belgium [France] with regard to which the parties are in conflict as to their respective rights, and which it may not be possible to settle amicably by the normal methods of diplomacy, shall be submitted for decision either to an arbitral tribunal or to the Permanent Court of International Justice, as laid down hereafter. It is agreed that the disputes referred to above include in particular those mentioned in article 13 of the Covenant of the League of Nations.

This provision does not apply to disputes arising out of events prior to the present convention and belonging to the past.

Disputes for the settlement of which a special procedure is laid down in other conventions in force between Germany and Belgium [France] shall be settled in conformity with the provisions of those conventions.

Article 2.   Before any resort is made to arbitral procedure or to procedure before the Permanent Court of International Justice, the dispute may, by agreement between the parties, be submitted, with a view to amicable settlement, to a permanent international commission styled the Permanent Conciliation Commission, constituted in accordance with the present convention.

Article 3.   In the case of a dispute the occasion of which, according to the municipal law of one of the parties, falls within the competence of the national courts of such party, the matter in dispute shall not be submitted to the procedure laid down in the present convention until a judgement with final effect has been pronounced, within a reasonable time, by the competent national judicial authority.

THE LOCARNO PACT 213

Article 4. The Permanent Conciliation Commission mentioned in article 2 shall be composed of five members, who shall be appointed as follows, that is to say: the German Government and the Belgian [French] Government shall each nominate a commissioner chosen from among their respective nationals, and shall appoint, by common agreement, the three other commissioners from among the nationals of third Powers: these three commissioners must be of different nationalities, and the German and Belgian [French] Governments shall appoint the president of the commission from among them.

The commissioners are appointed for three years, and their mandate is renewable. Their appointment shall continue until their replacement and, in any case, until the termination of the work in hand at the moment of the expiry of their mandate.

Vacancies which may occur as a result of death, resignation or any other cause shall be filled within the shortest possible time in the manner fixed for the nominations.

Article 5. The Permanent Conciliation Commission shall be constituted within three months from the entry into force of the present convention.

If the nomination of the commissioners to be appointed by common agreement should not have taken place within the said period, or, in the case of the filling of a vacancy, within three months from the time when the seat falls vacant, the President of the Swiss Confederation shall, in the absence of other agreement, be requested to make the necessary appointments.

Article 6. The Permanent Conciliation Commission shall be informed by means of a request addressed to the president by the two parties acting in agreement or, in the absence of such agreement, by one or other of the parties.

The request, after having given a summary account of the subject of the dispute, shall contain the invitation to the commission to take all necessary measures with a view to arrive at an amicable settlement.

If the request emanates from only one of the parties,

notification thereof shall be made without delay to the other
party.

Article 7.   Within fifteen days from the date when the
German Government or the Belgian [French] Government
shall have brought a dispute before the Permanent Conciliation Commission either party may, for the examination
of the particular dispute, replace its commissioner by a
person possessing special competence in the matter.

The party making use of this right shall immediately inform the other party; the latter shall in that case be entitled
to take similar action within fifteen days from the date
when the notification reaches it.

Article 8.   The task of the Permanent Conciliation Commission shall be to elucidate questions in dispute, to collect
with that object all necessary information by means of inquiry or otherwise, and to endeavour to bring the parties
to an agreement. It may, after the case has been examined,
inform the parties of the terms of settlement which seem
suitable to it, and lay down a period within which they
are to make their decision.

At the close of its labours the commission shall draw up
a report stating, as the case may be, either that the parties
have come to an agreement and, if need arises, the terms
of the agreement, or that it has been impossible to effect
a settlement.

The labours of the commission must, unless the parties
otherwise agree, be terminated within six months from the
day on which the commission shall have been notified of
the dispute.

Article 9.   Failing any special provision to the contrary,
the Permanent Conciliation Commission shall lay down its
own procedure, which in any case must provide for both
parties being heard. In regard to inquiries the commission,
unless it decides unanimously to the contrary, shall act in
accordance with the provisions of Chapter III (International Commissions of Inquiry) of the Hague Convention
of the 18th October, 1907, for the Pacific Settlement of
International Disputes.

Article 10. The Permanent Conciliation Commission shall meet, in the absence of agreement by the parties to the contrary, at a place selected by its president.

Article 11. The labours of the Permanent Conciliation Commission are not public, except when a decision to that effect has been taken by the commission with the consent of the parties.

Article 12. The parties shall be represented before the Permanent Conciliation Commission by agents, whose duty it shall be to act as intermediary between them and the commission; they may, moreover, be assisted by counsel and experts appointed by them for that purpose, and request that all persons whose evidence appears to them useful should be heard.

The commission, on its side, shall be entitled to request oral explanations from the agents, counsel and experts of the two parties, as well as from all persons it may think useful to summon with the consent of their Government.

Article 13. Unless otherwise provided in the present convention, the decisions of the Permanent Conciliation Commission shall be taken by a majority.

Article 14. The German and Belgian [French] Governments undertake to facilitate the labours of the Permanent Conciliation Commission and particularly to supply it to the greatest possible extent with all relevant documents and information, as well as to use the means at their disposal to allow it to proceed in their territory and in accordance with their law to the summoning and hearing of witnesses or experts, and to visit the localities in question.

Article 15. During the labours of the Permanent Conciliation Commission each commissioner shall receive salary, the amount of which shall be fixed by agreement between the German and Belgian [French] Governments, each of which shall contribute an equal share.

Article 16.   In the event of no amicable agreement being reached before the Permanent Conciliation Commission
the dispute shall be submitted by means of a special agreement either to the Permanent Court of International Justice
under the conditions and according to the procedure laid
down by its statute or to an arbitral tribunal under the
conditions and according to the procedure laid down by the
Hague Convention of the 18th October, 1907, for the
Pacific Settlement of International Disputes.

If the parties cannot agree on the terms of the special
agreement after a month's notice one or other of them may
bring the dispute before the Permanent Court of International Justice by means of an application.

Part II

Article 17.   All questions on which the German and
Belgian [French] Governments shall differ without being
able to reach an amicable solution by means of the normal
methods of diplomacy the settlement of which cannot be
attained by means of a judicial decision as provided in
article 1 of the present convention, and for the settlement
of which no procedure has been laid down by other conventions in force between the parties, shall be submitted
to the Permanent Conciliation Commission, whose duty it
shall be to propose to the parties an acceptable solution
and in any case to present a report.

The procedure laid down in articles 6–15 of the present
convention shall be applicable.

Article 18.   If the two parties have not reached an agreement within a month from the termination of the labours
of the Permanent Conciliation Commission the question
shall, at the request of either party, be brought before the
Council of the League of Nations, which shall deal with
it in accordance with article 15 of the Covenant of the
League.

General Provisions

Article 19. In any case, and particularly if the question on which the parties differ arises out of acts already committed or on the point of commission, the Conciliation Commission or, if the latter has not been notified thereof, the arbitral tribunal or the Permanent Court of International Justice, acting in accordance with article 41 of its statute, shall lay down within the shortest possible time the provisional measure to be adopted. It shall similarly be the duty of the Council of the League of Nations, if the question is brought before it, to ensure that suitable provisional measures are taken. The German and Belgian [French] Governments undertake respectively to accept such measures, to abstain from all measures likely to have a repercussion prejudicial to the execution of the decision or to the arrangements proposed by the Conciliation Commission or by the Council of the League of Nations, and in general to abstain from any sort of action whatsoever which may aggravate or extend the dispute.

Article 20. The present convention continues applicable as between Germany and Belgium [France] even when other Powers are also interested in the dispute.

Article 21. The present convention shall be ratified. Ratifications shall be deposited at Geneva with the League of Nations at the same time as the ratifications of the treaty concluded this day between Germany, Belgium, France, Great Britain, and Italy.

It shall enter into and remain in force under the same conditions as the said treaty.

The present convention, done in a single copy, shall be deposited in the archives of the League of Nations, the Secretary-General of which shall be requested to transmit certified copies to each of the two contracting Governments.

Done at Locarno, the 16th October, 1925.

STR.

E. V. [A. B.]

(4) Annexes D and E: Arbitration Treaties Between Germany and Poland and Between Germany and Czechoslovakia[3] (Translation)

The President of the German Empire and the President of the Polish [Czechoslovak] Republic

Equally resolved to maintain peace between Germany and Poland [Czechoslovakia] by assuring the peaceful settlement of differences which might arise between the two countries;

Declaring that respect for the rights established by treaty or resulting from the law of nations is obligatory for international tribunals;

Agreeing to recognize that the rights of a State cannot be modified save with its consent;

And considering that sincere observance of the methods of peaceful settlement of international disputes permits of resolving, without recourse to force, questions which may become the cause of division between States;

Have decided to embody in a treaty their common intentions in this respect, and have named as their plenipotentiaries the following: [names omitted]

Who, having exchanged their full powers, found in good and due form, are agreed upon the following articles:—

Part I

Article 1.   All disputes of every kind between Germany and Poland [Czechoslovakia] with regard to which the parties are in conflict as to their respective rights, and which it may not be possible to settle amicably by the normal methods of diplomacy, shall be submitted for decision either to an arbitral tribunal or to the Permanent Court of International Justice, as laid down hereafter. It is agreed that the disputes referred to above include in particular those mentioned in article 13 of the Covenant of the League of Nations.

[3] The terms of these treaties are identical.

This provision does not apply to disputes arising out of events prior to the present treaty and belonging to the past.

Disputes for the settlement of which a special procedure is laid down in other conventions in force between the high contracting parties shall be settled in conformity with the provisions of those conventions.

Article 2.   Before any resort is made to arbitral procedure or to procedure before the Permanent Court of International Justice, the dispute may, by agreement between the parties, be submitted, with a view to amicable settlement, to a permanent international commission, styled the Permanent Conciliation Commission, constituted in accordance with the present treaty.

Article 3.   In the case of a dispute the occasion of which, according to the municipal law of one of the parties, falls within the competence of the national courts of such party, the matter in dispute shall not be submitted to the procedure laid down in the present treaty until a judgement with final effect has been pronounced, within a reasonable time, by the competent national judicial authority.

Article 4.   The Permanent Conciliation Commission mentioned in article 2 shall be composed of five members, who shall be appointed as follows, that is to say: the high contracting parties shall each nominate a commissioner chosen from among their respective nationals, and shall appoint, by common agreement, the three other commissioners from among the nationals of third Powers; those three commissioners must be of different nationalities, and the high contracting parties shall appoint the president of the commission from among them.

The commissioners are appointed for three years, and their mandate is renewable. Their appointment shall continue until their replacement, and in any case until the termination of the work in hand at the moment of the expiry of their mandate.

Vacancies which may occur as a result of death, resignation or any other cause shall be filled within the shortest possible time in the manner fixed for the nominations.

Article 5.   The Permanent Conciliation Commission shall be constituted within three months from the entry into force of the present convention.

If the nomination of the commissioners to be appointed by common agreement should not have taken place within the said period, or, in the case of the filling of a vacancy, within three months from the time when the seat falls vacant, the President of the Swiss Confederation shall, in the absence of other agreement, be requested to make the necessary appointments.

Article 6.   The Permanent Conciliation Commission shall be informed by means of a request addressed to the president by the two parties acting in agreement, or, in the absence of such agreement, by one or other of the parties.

The request, after having given a summary account of the subject of the dispute, shall contain the invitation to the commission to take all necessary measures with a view to arrive at an amicable settlement.

If the request emanates from only one of the parties, notification thereof shall be made without delay to the other party.

Article 7.   Within fifteen days from the date when one of the high contracting parties shall have brought a dispute before the Permanent Conciliation Commission, either party may, for the examination of the particular dispute, replace its commissioner by a person possessing special competence in the matter.

The party making use of this right shall immediately inform the other party; the latter shall in that case be entitled to take similar action within fifteen days from the date when the notification reaches it.

Article 8.   The task of the Permanent Conciliation Commission shall be to elucidate questions in dispute, to collect with that object all necessary information by means of inquiry or otherwise, and to endeavour to bring the parties to an agreement. It may, after the case has been examined, inform the parties of the terms of settlement which seem suitable to it, and lay down a period within which they are to make their decision.

At the close of its labours the commission shall draw up a report stating, as the case may be, either that the parties have come to an agreement and, if need arises, the terms of the agreement, or that it has been impossible to effect a settlement.

The labours of the commission must, unless the parties otherwise agree, be terminated within six months from the day on which the commission shall have been notified of the dispute.

Article 9.   Failing any special provision to the contrary, the Permanent Conciliation Commission shall lay down its own procedure, which in any case must provide for both parties being heard. In regard to inquiries, the commission, unless it decides unanimously to the contrary, shall act in accordance with the provisions of Chapter III (International Commissions of Inquiry) of the Hague Convention of the 18th October, 1907, for the Pacific Settlement of International Disputes.

Article 10.   The Permanent Conciliation Commission shall meet, in the absence of agreement by the parties to the contrary, at a place selected by its president.

Article 11.   The labours of the Permanent Conciliation Commission are not public except when a decision to that effect has been taken by the commission with the consent of the parties.

Article 12.   The parties shall be represented before the Permanent Conciliation Commission by agents, whose duty it shall be to act as intermediary between them and the commission; they may moreover be assisted by counsel and experts appointed by them for that purpose, and request that all persons whose evidence appears to them useful should be heard.

The commission on its side shall be entitled to request oral explanations from the agents, counsel and experts of the two parties, as well as from all persons it may think useful to summon with the consent of their Government.

Article 13.   Unless otherwise provided in the present treaty the decisions of the Permanent Conciliation Commission shall be taken by a majority.

Article 14.   The high contracting parties undertake to facilitate the labours of the Permanent Conciliation Commission, and particularly to supply it to the greatest possible extent with all relevant documents and information, as well as to use the means at their disposal to allow it to proceed in their territory and in accordance with their law to the summoning and hearing of witnesses or experts, and to visit the localities in question.

Article 15.   During the labours of the Permanent Conciliation Commission each commissioner shall receive salary, the amount of which shall be fixed by agreement between the high contracting parties, each of which shall contribute an equal share.

Article 16.   In the event of no amicable agreement being reached before the Permanent Conciliation Commission the dispute shall be submitted by means of a special agreement either to the Permanent Court of International Justice under the conditions and according to the procedure laid down by its statute or to an arbitral tribunal under the conditions and according to the procedure laid down by the Hague Convention of the 18th October, 1907, for the Pacific Settlement of International Disputes.

If the parties cannot agree on the terms of the special agreement after a month's notice one or other of them may bring the dispute before the Permanent Court of International Justice by means of an application.

Part II

Article 17. All questions on which the German and Polish [Czechoslovak] Governments shall differ without being able to reach an amicable solution by means of the normal methods of diplomacy, the settlement of which cannot be attained by means of a judicial decision as provided in article 1 of the present treaty, and for the settlement of which no procedure has been laid down by other conventions in force between the parties shall be submitted to the Permanent Conciliation Commission, whose duty it shall be to propose to the parties an acceptable solution and in any case to present a report.

The procedure laid down in articles 6–15 of the present treaty shall be applicable.

Article 18. If the two parties have not reached an agreement within a month from the termination of the labours of the Permanent Conciliation Commission the question shall, at the request of either party, be brought before the Council of the League of Nations, which shall deal with it in accordance with article 15 of the Covenant of the League.

General Provisions

Article 19. In any case, and particularly if the question on which the parties differ arises out of acts already committed or on the point of commission, the Conciliation Commission or, if the latter has not been notified thereof, the arbitral tribunal or the Permanent Court of International Justice, acting in accordance with article 41 of its statute, shall lay down within the shortest possible time the provisional measures to be adopted. It shall similarly be the duty of the Council of the League of Nations, if the question is brought before it, to ensure that suitable provisional measures are taken. The high contracting parties undertake respectively to accept such measures, to abstain from all measures likely to have a repercussion prejudicial to the execution of the decision or to the arrangements proposed by the Conciliation Commission or by the Council of the League of Nations, and in general to abstain from any sort of action whatsoever which may aggravate or extend the dispute.

Article 20.   The present treaty continues applicable as between the high contracting parties even when other Powers are also interested in the dispute.

Article 21.   The present treaty, which is in conformity with the Covenant of the League of Nations, shall not in any way affect the rights and obligations of the high contracting parties as members of the League of Nations and shall not be interpreted as restricting the duty of the League to take whatever action may be deemed wise and effectual to safeguard the peace of the world.

Article 22.   The present treaty shall be ratified. Ratifications shall be deposited at Geneva with the League of Nations at the same time as the ratifications of the treaty concluded this day between Germany, Belgium, France, Great Britain, and Italy.

It shall enter into and remain in force under the same conditions as the said treaty.

The present treaty, done in a single copy, shall be deposited in the archives of the League of Nations, the Secretary-General of which shall be requested to transmit certified copies to each of the high contracting parties.

Done at Locarno, the 16th October, 1925.

STR.

(A. S.) [Dr. B.]

(5) Annex F: Draft Collective Note to Germany Regarding Article 16 of the League of Nations (Translation)

The German delegation has requested certain explanations in regard to article 16 of the Covenant of the League of Nations.

We are not in a position to speak in the name of the League, but in view of the discussions which have already taken place in the Assembly and in the commissions of the League of Nations, and after the explanations which have been exchanged between ourselves, we do not hesitate to inform you of the interpretation which, in so far as we are concerned, we place upon article 16.

In accordance with that interpretation the obligations resulting from the said article on the members of the League must be understood to mean that each State member of the League is bound to co-operate loyally and effectively in support of the Covenant and in resistance to any act of aggression to an extent which is compatible with its military situation and takes its geographical position into account.

E. V.   A. B.   A. C.   B. M.
Dr. B.   A. S.

(6) Treaties Between France and Poland and Between France and Czechoslovakia[4] (Translation)

The President of the French Republic and the President of the Polish [Czechoslovak] Republic;

Equally desirous to see Europe spared from war by a sincere observance of the undertakings arrived at this day with a view to the maintenance of general peace;

Have resolved to guarantee their benefits to each other reciprocally by a treaty concluded within the framework

[4] The terms of these treaties are identical.

of the Covenant of the League of Nations and of the treaties existing between them;

And have to this effect nominated for their plenipotentiaries: [names omitted]

Who, after having exchanged their full powers, found in good and due form, have agreed on the following provisions:—

Article 1.   In the event of Poland [Czechoslovakia] or France suffering from a failure to observe the undertakings arrived at this day between them and Germany with a view to the maintenance of general peace, France, and reciprocally Poland [Czechoslovakia], acting in application of article 16 of the Covenant of the League of Nations, undertake to lend each other immediately aid and assistance, if such a failure is accompanied by an unprovoked recourse to arms.

In the event of the Council of the League of Nations, when dealing with a question brought before it in accordance with the said undertakings, being unable to succeed in making its report accepted by all its members other than the representatives of the parties to the dispute, and in the event of Poland [Czechoslovakia] or France being attacked without provocation, France, or reciprocally Poland [Czechoslovakia], acting in application of article 15, paragraph 7, of the Covenant of the League of Nations, will immediately lend aid and assistance.

Article 2.   Nothing in the present treaty shall affect the rights and obligations of the high contracting parties as members of the League of Nations, or shall be interpreted as restricting the duty of the League to take whatever action may be deemed wise and effectual to safeguard the peace of the world.

Article 3.   The present treaty shall be registered with the League of Nations in accordance with the Covenant.

Article 4.   The present treaty shall be ratified. The ratifications will be deposited at Geneva with the League of Nations at the same time as the ratification of the treaty concluded this day between Germany, Belgium, France, Great Britain and Italy, and the ratification of the treaty concluded at the same time between Germany and Poland.

It will enter into force and remain in force under the same conditions as the said treaties.

The present treaty done in a single copy will be deposited in the archives of the League of Nations, and the Secretary-General of the League will be requested to transmit certified copies to each of the high contracting parties.

Done at Locarno, the 16th October, 1925.

Bibliography

Collections of Documents

Commission de Publication des Documents Relatifs aux Origines de la Guerre, 1939–1945, *Documents Diplomatiques Français, 1932–1939* (Paris, 1963 ff.).

Documents on German Foreign Policy, 1918–1945 (Washington, D.C., 1949 ff.).

Foreign Relations of the United States (Washington, D.C., 1861 ff.).

International Military Tribunal, *Trial of the Major War Criminals before the International Military Tribunal, 1945–1946*, 42 vols. (Nuremberg, 1947–1949).

Nazi Conspiracy and Aggression, 8 vols. and 2 supplements (Washington, D.C.).

Royal Institute of International Affairs, *Documents on International Affairs* (New York, 1929 ff.).

Woodward, E. L., and R. Butler, eds., *Documents on British Foreign Policy, 1919–1939* (London, 1946 ff.).

Secondary Sources, Memoirs, and Articles

Angress, W. T., *Stillborn Revolution: The Communist Bid for Power in Germany, 1921–1923* (Princeton, 1963).

Ball, M. M., *Post-War German-Austrian Relations: The Anschluss Movement, 1918–1936* (Stanford, Calif., 1937).

Baynes, N. H., *The Speeches of Adolf Hitler, 1922–1939* (London, 1942).

Beck, J., *Final Report* (New York, 1957).

Beloff, M., "Soviet Foreign Policy, 1929–1941: Some Notes," *Soviet Studies* (October 1950).

Bennett, E. W., *Germany and the Diplomacy of the Financial Crisis 1931* (Cambridge, Mass., 1962).

Bonnet, G., *Défense de la Paix,* 2 vols. (Geneva, 1948).

———, *Le Quai d'Orsay sous Trois Républiques* (Paris, 1961).

Bretton, H. L., *Stresemann and the Revision of Versailles* (Stanford, Calif., 1953).

Brook-Shepard, G., *The Anschluss* (Philadelphia, 1963).

Budurowycz, B. B., *Polish-Soviet Relations, 1932–1939* (New York, 1963).

Bullock, A., *Hitler: A Study in Tyranny* (rev. ed., New York, 1964).

Cameron, E. R., *Prologue to Appeasement: A Study in French Foreign Policy* (Washington, D.C., 1942).

Carr, E. H., *German-Soviet Relations between the Two World Wars, 1919–1939* (Baltimore, 1951).

Carter, G. M., *The British Commonwealth and International Security: The Role of the Dominions, 1919–1939* (Toronto, 1947).

Castellan, A., *Le Réarmement Clandestin du Reich 1930–1935* (Paris, 1954).

Cattell, D., *Soviet Diplomacy and the Spanish Civil War* (Berkeley, Calif., 1957).

Churchill, W. S., *The Gathering Storm* (Boston, 1948).

Ciano, G., *Diaries, 1939–1943* (New York, 1946).

———, *Diplomatic Papers* (London, 1948).

———, *Hidden Diary, 1937–1938* (New York, 1953).

Clemenceau, G., *Grandeur and Misery of Victory* (New York, 1930).

Colvin, I., *None So Blind: A British Diplomatic View of the Origins of World War II* (New York, 1965).

Craig, G. A., *From Bismarck to Adenauer: Aspects of German Statecraft* (Baltimore, 1958).

———, *The Politics of the Prussian Army, 1640–1945* (New York, 1955; paperback ed., 1964).

———, and F. Gilbert, eds., *The Diplomats, 1919–1939* (Princeton, 1953; paperback ed., 2 vols., New York, 1963).

D'Abernon, V., *The Diary of an Ambassador,* 3 vols. (New York, 1929–1931).

Davies, J. E., *Mission to Moscow* (New York, 1941).

Debicki, R., *Foreign Policy of Poland 1919–1939* (New York, 1962).

De la Gorce, P. M., *The French Army: A Military-Political History* (New York, 1963).

Dodd, W. E., *Diary: 1933–1938* (New York, 1941).

Eden, A. (Earl of Avon), *Facing the Dictators* (Boston, 1962).

Erickson, J., *The Soviet High Command: A Military-Political History, 1918–1941* (New York, 1962).

Eubank, K., *Munich* (Norman, Okla., 1963).

Eyck, E., *A History of the Weimar Republic,* 2 vols. (Cambridge, Mass., 1962, 1963).

Feiling, K., *The Life of Neville Chamberlain* (London, 1946).

Flandin, P., *Politique Française: 1919–1947* (Paris, 1947).

François-Poncet, A., *The Fateful Years: Memoirs of a French Ambassador in Berlin, 1931–1938* (London, 1949).

Furnia, A. H., *The Diplomacy of Appeasement: Anglo-French Relations and the Prelude to World War II, 1931–1938* (Washington, D.C., 1960).

Gafencu, G., *Last Days of Europe: A Diplomatic Journey in 1939* (New Haven, Conn., 1948).

Gasiorowski, Z. J., "The German-Polish Nonagression Pact of 1934," *Journal of Central European Affairs* (April 1955).

Gathorne-Hardy, G. M., *A Short History of International Affairs, 1920–1939,* 4th ed. (London, 1950).

Gatzke, H. W., "Gustav Stresemann: A Bibliographical Article," *Journal of Modern History* (March 1964).

———, "Russo-German Military Collaboration during the Weimar Republic," *American Historical Review,* Vol. LXIII, No. 3.

———, "The Stresemann Papers," *Journal of Modern History* (March 1954).

———, *Stresemann and the Rearmament of Germany* (Baltimore, 1954).

George, M., *The Warped Vision: British Foreign Policy 1933–1939* (Pittsburgh, 1965).

Gilbert, M., *Plough My Own Furrow: The Story of Lord Allen of Hurtwood* (London, 1965).

———, and R. Gott, *The Appeasers* (Boston, 1963).

Gorlitz, W., *History of the German General Staff* (New York, 1953).

Hallgarten, G. W. F., "General Hans von Seeckt and Russia, 1920–1922," *Journal of Modern History* (March 1949).

Halperin, S. W., *Germany Tried Democracy: A Political History of the Reich from 1918–1933* (Hamden, Conn., 1963).

Henderson, N., *Failure of a Mission: Berlin, 1937–1939* (London, 1940).

Herriot, E., *Jadis. Vol. II: D'une Guerre a l'autre, 1914–1936* (Paris, 1952).

Hilger, G., and A. G. Meyer, *The Incompatible Allies—A Memoir-History of German Soviet Relations 1918–1941* (New York, 1953).

Hitler, A., *Mein Kampf* trans., R. Manheim (Boston, Sentry ed., 1943).

Kennedy, J. F., *Why England Slept* (New York, 1940; paperback ed., 1962).

King, J. C., *Foch Versus Clemenceau: France and German Dismemberment, 1918–1919* (Cambridge, Mass., 1960).

Klein, B. H., *Germany's Economic Preparations for War* (Cambridge, Mass., 1959).

Korbel, J., *Poland between East and West* (Princeton, 1963).

Langer, W. L., and S. E. Gleason, *The Challenge to Isolation*, 2 vols. (New York, 1952).

Liddell Hart, B. H., *The Liddell Hart Memoirs 1895–1938,* Vol. I (New York, 1965).

Luža, R., *The Transfer of the Sudeten Germans: A Study of Czech-German Relations, 1933–1962* (New York, 1964).

Macleod, I., *Neville Chamberlain* (London, 1961).

McRandle, J. H., *The Track of the Wolf: Essays on National Socialism and Its Leader, Adolf Hitler* (Evanston, Ill., 1965).

Medlicott, W. N., ed., *From Metternich to Hitler: Aspects of British and Foreign History, 1840–1939* (New York, 1963).

Micaud, C. A., *The French Right and Nazi Germany 1937–1939* (New York, 1943).

Miller, D. H., *The Geneva Protocol* (New York, 1925).

Milward, A. S., *The German Economy at War* (London, 1965).

Morgan, J. H., *Assize of Arms: The Disarmament of Germany and her Rearmament, 1919–1939* (New York, 1946).

Morrow, F. D., *The Peace Settlement in the German Polish Borderlands* (London, 1936).

Namier, L. B., *Diplomatic Prelude, 1938–1939* (London, 1948).

———, *Europe in Decay: A Study in Disintegration* (London, 1950).

Neumann, F. L., *Behemoth: The Structure and Practice of National Socialism 1933–1944* (Toronto, New York, 1942).

Nicolson, H., *Curzon: The Last Phase, 1919–1925* (New York, 1939).

Noel-Baker, P. J., *The Geneva Protocol for the Pacific Settlement of International Disputes* (London, 1925).

Nogueres, H., *Munich: "Peace for our Time"* (New York, 1965).

Nolte, E., *Three Faces of Fascism* (London, 1965).

Paul-Boncour, J., *Entre Deux Guerres: Souvenirs sur la III Republique,* Vols. II and III (Paris, 1945–1946).

Petrie, Sir C., *Life and Letters of the Right Honorable Sir Austen Chamberlain,* 2 vols. (London, 1939–1940).

Puzzo, D. A., *Spain and the Great Powers, 1936–1941* (New York, 1962).

Rauschning, H., *Hitler Speaks* (London, 1939).

———, *The Voice of Destruction* (New York, 1940).

Renouvin, P., ed., *Histoire des Relations Internationales,* Vol. 7, *Les Crises du xxᵉ Siècle: De 1914 à 1929* (Paris, 1957); Vol. 8, *Les Crises du xxᵉ Siècle: De 1929 à 1945* (Paris, 1958).

Rouse, A. L., *Appeasement: A Study in Political Decline, 1933–1939* (New York, 1963).

Royal Institute of International Affairs, *Survey of International Affairs* (London, 1925 ff.).

Salvemini, G., *Prelude to World War II* (New York, 1954).

Scheele, G., *The Weimar Republic* (London, 1946).

Schmidt, P., *Hitler's Interpreter* (London, 1951).

Schuman, F. L., *Europe on the Eve: The Crisis of Diplomacy, 1933–1939* (New York, 1939).

———, *Night over Europe: The Diplomacy of Nemesis, 1939–1940* (New York, 1941).

———, *War and Diplomacy in the French Republic* (New York, 1931).

Schweitzer, A., *Big Business in the Third Reich* (Bloomington, Ind., 1964).

Scott, W. E., *Alliance Against Hitler: The Origins of the Franco-Soviet Pact* (Durham, N.C., 1962).

Selsam, J. P., *The Attempts to Form an Anglo-French Alliance: 1919–1924* (Philadelphia, 1936).

Seton-Watson, H., *Eastern Europe between the Wars, 1918–1941* (Cambridge, England, 1946).

Sutton, E., ed. and trans., *Gustav Stresemann: His Diaries, Letters, and Papers,* 3 vols. (New York, 1935–1940).

Taylor, A. J. P., *The Origins of the Second World War* (New York, 1962).

Thomas, H., *The Spanish Civil War* (New York, 1963).

Trevor-Roper, H. R., ed., *Blitzkrieg to Defeat: Hitler's War Directives 1939–1945* (New York, 1965).

Turner, H. A., Jr., *Stresemann and the Politics of the Weimar Republic* (Princeton, 1963).

Von Manstein, E., *Lost Victories* (Chicago, 1958).

Von Rabenau, F., *Seecht: Aus Seinen Leben* (Leipzig, 1940).

Walters, F. P., *A History of the League of Nations,* 2 vols. (London, 1952).

Wandycz, P. S., *France and Her Eastern Allies, 1919–1925: French-Czechoslovak-Polish Relations from the Paris Peace Conference to Locarno* (Minneapolis, 1962).

Watkins, K. W., *Britain Divided: The Effect of the Spanish Civil War on British Public Opinion* (London, 1963).

Watt, D. C., "The Anglo-German Naval Agreement of 1935: An Interim Judgement," *Journal of Modern History* (June 1956).

————, *Personalities and Politics: Studies in the Formulation of British Foreign Policy in the Twentieth Century* (Notre Dame, Ind., 1965).

————, "The Secret Laval-Mussolini Agreement of 1935 on Ethiopia," *The Middle East Journal* (Winter 1961).

Weinberg, G. L., "Hitler's Image of the United States," *American Historical Review* (July 1964).

Weizsäcker, E., *Memoirs* (Chicago, 1951).

Wheeler-Bennett, J. W., *Munich: Prologue to Tragedy* (New York, 1948).

————, *The Nemesis of Power: The German Army in Politics, 1918–1945* (2d ed., London, 1964).

Wolfers, A., *Britain and France between Two Wars: Conflicting Strategies of Peace since Versailles* (New York, 1940).

Wrench, Sir E., *Geoffrey Dawson and Our Times* (London, 1955).

Index